Jean Delize

U-Boote
crews

Histoire & Collections

The heirs of the Great War. After the *status quo* of the Battle of Jutland, the big ships of the Hochseeflotte were blockaded in the damp bay of the gulf of Bremen. The undefeated submarine arm was the only one capable of carrying on the fight. *(DR)*

When the last ships of the Hochsee Flotte were scuttled at Scapa Flow in 1919, it seemed like the irreversible end of the Kriegsmarine. The victorious Allies at the end of the Paris Peace Conference at Versailles left no doubt as to the role now assigned to it ; the overall tonnage could not exceed 108,000 metric tons and its manpower was limited to 15,000 men, confining it to the role of coast-guard in the Baltic. Even though later, its overall tonnage was increased to 144,000 Washington metric tons (1 Washington ton was the equivalent of 1,016 metric tons), it remained without its ocean going element during the 1920s. The latter made its return with the construction of pocket battleships at the beginning of the 1930s. However, it was not until June 1935 that the submarine arm made its return, an arm that, thanks to its successes at the end of the Great War, had allowed the Kriegsmarine, blockaded in the Bremen triangle and condemned to the role of « fleet in being », to record its first successes.

Despite these successes in 1918, the submarines were far from being considered as the glory of the German Navy. The Navy had lost its prestige with the mutinies that broke out in the major ports, leading to the fall of the regime and giving weight to the « stabbed in the back » theory. The submarines (unaffected by the mutinies, as were all the other small ships) were victims of their success. Because of the total war that they had waged against Allied shipping, they were seen as being the cause of America's entry into the war and therefore responsible for the final defeat. The feeling that the submarine was a weapon of piracy, unfit for civilised nations, was so widespread that

above
The U-Boote War Badge instituted in 1918 by the Emperor William II.
(Militaria Magazine)

below
Submarine studies at a naval academy. The entire machinery of a submersible has been installed for the use of the trainees. *(DR)*

Following page below
An American destroyer. The development of ASDIC by the British and Americans meant that the submarines were doomed to become the prey of this type of escort vessel.
(DR)

hardly anyone bothered about the clause in the Treaty of Versailles that banned the Germans from building them. The French had to fiercely resist the Anglo-Saxon pressure, to avoid submarines being simply considered as outlawed during the international disarmament conference that took place in Washington during the winter of 1921-1922. The submarine would, at least, have to conform to the « rules of engagement » (the German implementation of the international laws governing the inspection and the capture of merchant shipping), that laid down so many restrictions on the submarine as to render its tactical advantages useless. Germany put its signature to this arrangement in November 1936 in London. When attacking merchant shipping, submarines would now have to act as surface vessels.

Consequently, according to the « rules of engagement », the submarine would have to surface in order to stop and inspect a merchant ship. If the latter could be proven to be legally sinkable, the submarine would have to ensure the safety of the crew. In the agreement of 1936, lifeboats were not considered as being safe, the submarine would have to take the crew onboard or renounce the sinking of the ship. Thus condemned to the role of a surface ship when attacking merchant shipping, the submarine was rendered impotent and vulnerable to immediate destruction, especially given the Anglo-Saxon development of ASDIC (Allied Submarine Detection Investigation Committee), an ultrasonic submarine detection device, the ancestor of Sonar, which seemed to condemn the submarine to the role of prey for escorts that were heavily armed with depth

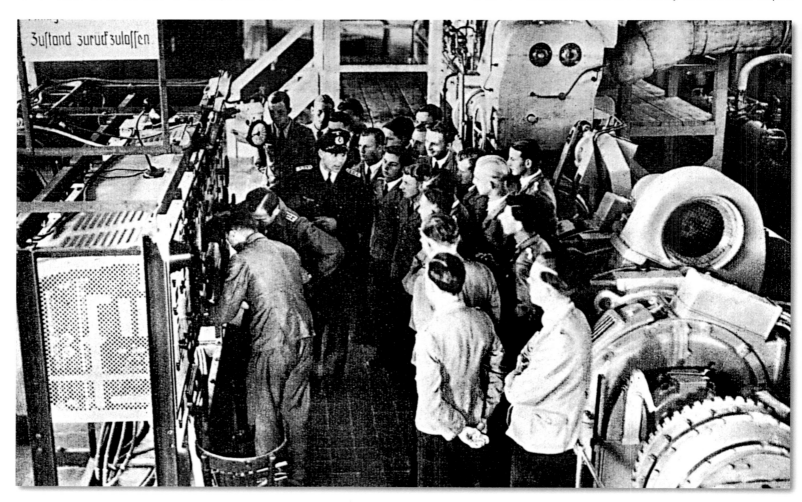

A Type II U-Boot on a pre-war exercise in the Baltic Sea. *(DR)*

charges. Despite this generalised disgrace, a few German officers and political leaders remained convinced of the usefulness of this weapon whose immense possibilities the First World War had shown. To give up on it without any hope of a return, seemed at this time, suicidal.

This was the reason why, in 1922, Doctor Hans Techel, helped by a team made up of submarine specialists, went to Holland, with plans taken from the Krupp Germania naval shipyards, so that they would avoid the investigations of the Inter-Allied Disarmament Commission. Under the direction of the Dutch research department, Ingenieurskantoor voor Scheepsbouw, Germany was able to maintain a high level of knowledge in the field of the submarine. Although now building for others and outside of Germany, it was German personnel that, under the guise of training foreign crews, maintained a high level of

A sailor's cap inspired by the 1914-1918 issued model.
(P-M. Rousseau collection)

the precious knowledge acquired during the previous conflict. In this way, in the summer of 1930, the first German submariners trained on a 500-ton Finnish submarine that officially only carried tourists...

As early as 1925, the need to keep the information learned during the First

TEXT OF THE 1936 TREATY

« *The signatory powers wish to make more effective the rules adopted by the civilised nations for the protection of the lives of neutral nations and non-fighting elements at sea in wartime, declaring that amongst these rules, the following should be considered as being an integral part of international law.*

...Before a merchant ship can be seized, it must have received the order to submit itself to a visit and inspection in view of determining its character. It is forbidden to attack a merchant ship, unless it refuses to undergo a visit and inspection after receiving the order or refusing to obey the order. After being seized, it is forbidden to destroy the ship before the crew and passengers have been made safe.

...Belligerent submarines are in no circumstances exempt from the rules mentioned above. In the case of a submarine being unable to seize a merchant ship by respecting these rules, the known rights of the people force it to give up on the attack and the seizure and to allow the merchant ship to continue its route without being molested... »

World War on German soil, was seen as obvious by veteran submariners, who began putting together the first theoretical training programmes under the authority of Admiral Spindler.

The latter, after having been put in charge of the special department AU (Ausbildung : training), dedicated to submersibles, put together a series of theoretical lessons at the torpedo and transmissions school of Flensburg-Mürwick. Using films taken on board U-35 and U-133 during the war, 24 midshipmen were able to learn about the origins of the submarine as a weapon, foreign submarines and the basics of weaponry and attack tactics.

The training remained in this basic form, without any real practical objective, until October 1933, the date when Admiral Von Blomberg created the new submarine school at Kiel. This is the reason why only 17 out of the 167 officers of the 1934 Naval College promotion served aboard submarines in 1937, due to a lack of serious training in their years of apprenticeship. Before the middle of the thirties, we estimate that midshipmen received only a week of submarine training. The school was commanded by Fregattenkapitän Karl Slevogt and the school began teaching in the summer of 1933, with lessons given by veteran submarine commanders. Lessons in the theory of submarine construction and the launching of torpedoes were followed by more practical lessons.

On board a minesweeper, equipped with a simulator, the future crews put the finishing touches to their knowledge of instruments. The simulator allowed them to train in the use of the periscope, a replica having been installed in a compartment on the deck. As well as this, other control instruments were replicated in a control room, whilst a replica of a Type II motor allowed the engine crew personnel to perfect their knowledge of the propulsion systems. The simulators were then improved, such as the F-Gerät (Fahrt-Gerät or patrol device) used at Neustadt. Placed inside a full sized conning tower, the future commander could see, through his periscope, miniature ships moving at varying speed, operated by a civilian. Light and sea conditions could be modified in order to simulate a day or night attack in a calm or heavy sea. On completion of 15 victorious attacks using this device, the trainee could then claim to have « patrolled with Barkow », this being the name of the civilian operating the miniature ships.

From 1932, Admiral Raeder set up a plan to create three submarine semi flotillas. Equipment was imported from Spanish, Dutch and Finnish shipyards and stored at the Kiel shipyards. In the autumn of 1934, there were enough periscopes, diesels and electric motors and spare parts to build ten submarines in Germany where the naval shipyards were simply waiting for the authorisation to begin building again. This happened in June 1935 with the German-British agreement that authorised the development of a German surface fleet to 35 % of the British fleet and that of a submarine fleet equivalent to 45 % (24,000 Washington metric tons), which became 100 % after re-negotiations. Construction could now begin and the 24 coastal submarines and two ocean going submarines that underwent construction

In September 1935, the first training flotilla comprised the first six U-Boote (U-1 to U-6). *(DR)*

above
Commander Weddigen, the German submarine « ace » of the First World War. Decorated here with the « Pour le Mérite », he remained famous in the memories of all the German submariners between the two wars, who wanted to equal his record of September 22nd, 1914 when he sunk in succession the three British cruisers, *HMS Aboukir*, *HMS Hogue*, and *HMS Cressy*. *(DR)*

following page above
An operator, placed behind scenery, actions and moves at differing speeds a model ship. *(DR)*

were completed by the naval shipyards of Deutsche-Werke and Germania-Werft at the end of the year. In the spring of 1936, the big Bremen shipyard, Deschimag AG, delivered two Type A1 vessels, followed by an accelerated construction programme which involved 16 naval shipyards in the construction of U-Boats.

From September 1935, the first training flotilla, comprising the first six U-Boote (U-1 to U-6), four old torpedo boats and a supply ship, was ready to get under way and to be attached to the school of submarine navigation, commanded by Slevogt. Each trainee submariner spent between four and twenty days at sea, undergoing exercises which added the finishing touches to what had been learnt in the classroom. At the same time, the first operational flotilla, named Weddigen (after one of the German « aces » of submarine warfare during the First World War), made up of 250-ton vessels (U-7 to U-9 to which were attached U-10 to U-18), was officially formed at Kiel. Korvettenkapitän (Commander) Karl Dönitz, who had just taken over the command, assisted by Chief Engineer Second Class Thedsen, put into place a six month period of training which aimed to make the submarine arm and its crews, the fighting arm of the German Navy, and the crews the elite personnel. It was this flotilla which carried out the first combat and torpedo exercises. This operational flotilla was rapidly joined by five more (Saltzwedel and Hundius based at Wilhelmshaven, Lohs, Emsmann and Wegener based at Kiel) increasing the German submarine fleet to 57 vessels put into service between 1935 and September 1939. ❒

above
Grossadmiral Karl Dönitz.
(ECPAD/DAM 1059 L12)

below
The Friedrich Krupp Germania Werft AG naval shipyards at Kiel were the biggest manufacturers of U-Boote. In terms of tonnage they were well ahead of the other North Sea shipyards (Deschimag AG of Bremen, Kriegsmarine Werft of Wilhelshaven, Howaldts Werke of Hamburg) and those of the Baltic Sea (Deutsche Werke of Kiel, Neptun Werft of Rostock or Schichau Werke of Danzig) They are shown here in September-October 1941.
(DR)

GROSSADMIRAL KARL DÖNITZ (1891-1980)

Having joined the Imperial Navy in 1910, he performed brilliantly in the submarine arm during the First World War, at the end of which he was captured whilst commanding U-68. In the years between the two wars, he was given the command of a torpedo boat flotilla where he perfected his knowledge of anti submarine warfare, something which would prove to be of great use in the training of his U-Boote commanders. In 1935, Grossadmiral Raeder decided to reform the submarine arm, the task of which was given to Captain Dönitz. The two men, however, were far from sharing the same points of view as to the potential of this arm. Dönitz was convinced that the war against trade links, led by submarines would be of use to Germany as a continental power. The latter's intuition was quickly confirmed and, on January 31st, 1943, he became the commander in Chief (Oberbefehlshaber) of the Navy. However, in spite of the hope that he placed in acoustic torpedoes and the schnorchel, and despite the appearance of the Type XXI and XXIII, he was incapable of curbing the powerful Allied war machine. In the last months of the war, his fighting zone was limited to the Baltic with the role of getting as many east German refugees as possible away from this region which was threatened by the Russian advance. Appointed as Hitler's successor after the latter's death, he maintained power until arrested by the Allies.

At the beginning of the war,
a U-Boot and destroyers take part
in exercises in the Baltic Sea.
(DR)

TRAINING AND ITS PRINCIPLES

THE TRAINING OF THE MEN AND THE MACHINE

When Dönitz took over the command of the 1st Flotilla of the re-born submarine branch, he was far from unknown. A veteran U-Boote « ace » of the First World War, thanks to his different postings within the surface navy during the twenties, he was able to see the best ways of countering and to check his intuitions concerning the best way of using its full potential.

Moreover, the British, using the same logic, placed the veteran submariner Max Horton, the admiral in charge of the Western Approaches, in charge of the anti-submarine measures. In order to be a good hunter, one had to know one's prey, and vice versa, the prey is even more redoubtable if it knows the tricks of its hunter.

right
**The 1938 model naval dagger.
The silver knot was worn by all
officers with the exception of
Kadetten and Fähnriche.
Admirals wore a gold knot.
In the same year, Grossadmiral
Raeder decided to create an
honour dagger derived from
this model. It was only awarded
seven times, for a glorious feat,
by Raeder himself, four times
for submariners: in 1940 for
Gunther Prien, in 1942 for
Erich Topp, Reinhard Suhren
and Albert Brandi. In 1943,
Dönitz only awarded one to a
U-Boot commander.**
(Militaria Magazine)

below
**An American convoy heading for
the Western Approaches.** *(DR)*

Tactical principles

The first problem Dönitz faced was the best way to exploit the potential of the submarine and the training of the crew in surface attacks; a tactic that needed the development of an offensive spirit. The first sign of this offensive spirit appeared in the

choice of firing as close as possible to the target. Before Dönitz, the rule was to keep at least 3,000 metres away and not risking being picked up by ASDIC, the performance of which was still an unknown quantity and very overestimated.

Dönitz, convinced that this device's potential was exaggerated, recommended the opposite, firing close up at a distance of less than 600 metres. Indeed, the submarine seemed an excel-

means that Dönitz had at his disposal were not sufficient to carry out the tactics, of which he had glimpsed the destructive possibilities. This weakness was compensated by a more advanced training and teaching programme. This choice was even more obvious in that it allowed men to become used to the sea conditions and navigating in an area that they would be called upon to operate in a future conflict. This intention of

lent surface torpedo boat, but with the advantage over the latter, apart from being able to disappear under water, of having a less visible outline at night : a submarine's outline being even more discreet the nearer it is, in the visual angle of warships or close merchant ships. Added to this advantage of invisibility that allowed for a surface attack was that of discretion ; ASDIC Type submarine detection devices picked up under water sound and were not able to detect the approach of a submarine on the surface.

However, for Dönitz, convincing people of what appeared to him as obvious was far from simple, and the first exercises did not prove him right. Indeed, the first tactical exercise involving a submarine and an ASDIC equipped escort in the Bay of Kiel in spring 1939, was a failure. The U-Boote were immediately detected before they could even launch a torpedo. Dönitz, however, was sure of his instinct, and repeated the exercise in the Baltic and the Skageraak in May and June of the same year. The submarines were this time successful and managed to remain undetected. Even if this success was due more to the Baltic currents than an obvious tactical superiority, these exercises motivated the Commanders and gave them absolute confidence in what their vessels could achieve. The

above
A four year naval service medal which belonged to a submariner.
(P-M. Rousseau collection)

AN EXTRACT FROM THE *ORGANISATION OF SUBMARINE WARFARE* BY DÖNITZ IN 1935

« *The submarine is essentially an attack weapon. Its great range makes it suitable for operations in far-off seas. Given its low speed, on surface and when submerged, its tactical mobility against rapid forces is fundamentally excluded. Its employment will, therefore, be in principle static.*
War missions entrusted to the U-Boote will depend on those assigned to the fleet. If we wage war against an enemy who does not depend on supplies from overseas, our submarines, contrary to what they accomplished between 1915 and 1918, will not have to wage a commercial war for which they are not suited because of their low speed. They will have to place themselves on alert, near the access channels to enemy ports, where the traffic is at its heaviest. Priority targets are enemy warships and troop carriers. »

keeping the U-Boote at sea for as long as possible, demanded the development of a fleet that was independent of all naval bases. This independence was made possible by a supply ship that carried everything necessary for the maintenance and repair of the fleet's vessels. A training programme was then set up, based on the multiplication of repetitive exercises, below and above surface. In this way, every U-Boot carried out 66 torpedo firing simulations, only using compressed air once to economize the expensive weapons. This was carried out on the surface as well as under water before beginning more complex tactical exercises. Next to follow were tactical night manoeuvres, those of escape, carrying out diurnal and nocturnal surface attack ; these were an essential part of the training. Far from being an end in itself, these exercises were a preliminary to the mission that the submarine would have to carry out in wartime.

From this repetitive training was born a specific tactic. Although they were essential trials for the crews, they also allowed for the trying out of the different theories that Dönitz began thinking of only from 1939, under the name of Rudeltaktik, the Wolf Pack tactic. Even though the foundations had certainly been laid when he took his command, the material means at his disposal had not allowed him to carry it out in the way he was able to in 1940.

This tactic was even more effective for being carried out at night, as this form of combat required very high qualities in those who were responsible for its execution. It seems that the night surface attack tactic was due more to the submarine commanders than

Dönitz himself who simply adapted and theorised it.

In order to back up the perfect mastery of the weapon, Dönitz sought to instil in his crews an offensive spirit that was a necessary component in the use of the submarine weapon. He demanded that in the case of convoys, the attack would be led, without any regard to danger, inside the enemy's defensive perimeter. This was in contradiction with the theory of the Neustadt U-Boote school on the Holstein coast.

This theory originated from the anti submarine school and stated that short distant attacks should be abandoned because of the improve-

OTTO KRETSCHMER
(1912-1998)

Having joined the German Navy at the age of 17, he spent three months on the sailing school ship *Niobé*, before joining the light cruiser *Emden* for a year's cruise apprenticeship. After having served on the light cruiser *Köln*, he joined the submarine arm in January 1936 and took command of U-35 with which he carried out patrol missions in Spanish waters in 1937. It was, however, with U-23 that he scored his first successes. Right from the beginning of the Second World War, he undertook patrols in the North Sea, along the English and Scottish coasts, before sinking, respectively in January and February 1940, the Danish tanker *Danmark* and the British destroyer *HMS Daring*. But it was with U-99 that he had his most spectacular successes and he became part of the German submariners' legend for his audacity and efficiency in night attacks against convoys, where he gloriously illustrated his motto « *one torpedo, one ship* ». At the end of 1940, « silent Otto » became the tonnage king with forty ships sunk, representing over 250,000 metric tons. During his last patrol, he sank no less than 10 Allied ships before being captured on March 17th, 1941, south east of Iceland by the destroyer *HMS Walker*. Imprisoned in Camp 30, Canada, he was freed in December 1947, a date from which, he was authorised to go back to Germany. In 1955, he joined the Bundesmarine, leaving in 1970 with the rank of Flottilleinadmiral. Here he proudly wears the Knight's Cross of the Iron Cross oak leaves and swords which he won on December 26,1941, a long time after this photo was taken, which explains why the photo was touched up by the propaganda department.

above
A convoy at berth ready to cast off under Royal Navy escort. Dönitz demanded that in the case of convoys, attacks were to be made, scorning danger, within the enemy's lines of security.
(DR)

above
A Kriegsmarine identity tag. 43 denotes the year of induction (1943).
(F. Bachmann collection)

above
Otto Kretschmer, nicknamed « Silent Otto » by his men.
(DR)

ment in defensive measures. The Wolf Pack theory was proved right, as seen with the successes scored by the « aces » in the years 1940-1941, the best example being that of the Commander Kretschmer. The « tonnage king » was convinced that an attack should be carried out within the defensive perimeter, in the very heart of the convoy lines.

The Wolf Pack tactic stemmed from these principles. Used for the first time in the autumn of 1937, during the big Wehrmacht manoeuvres, it rested on two essential principles, that of the centralised command on land, and the joint search for convoys. When a convoy was believed to be en route, the Wolf Pack would set up a stationary barrier in the path of the convoy. The submarines remained on the surface, on the limit of visibility between each other, roughly five miles (9,26 km), over a total distance of 30 miles (55,56 km). Once a convoy was spotted by a submarine, it would signal a short 20 letter message which included the convoy's position, heading, speed, number of vessels and warships, weather conditions and the submarine's fuel reserves. It would then discreetly track the convoy, remaining on the surface and waiting for other submarines to join so that a night attack could be launched.

When the attack was launched, however, it was by no means governed by a single commander, which in any case would have been impossible to do. Dönitz, following the example of Nelson, allowed his commanders to use their initiative. The submarines would position themselves for tracking the convoy following the directives set out by the future Grossadmiral, which directly gave his orders to his commanders, the latter then being quite free to change their positions according to their tactical

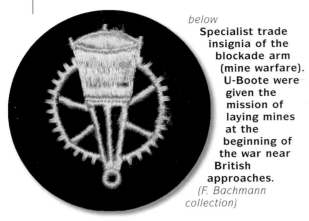

below
Specialist trade insignia of the blockade arm (mine warfare). U-Boote were given the mission of laying mines at the beginning of the war near British approaches.
(F. Bachmann collection)

A U-Boot seen from a twin engine Heinkel 111. *(DR)*

inspiration and the situation at the time. Even though the tactical foundations of the Wolf Pack were laid down from 1935 onwards, they were constantly enriched with the knowledge picked up from the first training exercises, before being assembled in a submarine commander's manual.

Generally speaking, the setting out of the principles of German submarine warfare, was done

THE GERMAN NAVY AND AVIATION

The use of submarines in the way imagined by Dönitz called for the support of a strong fleet air arm, something that he never had. Because of the personality of Reichsmarschall Göring, for whom « *all that flies belongs to us* », the German Navy could not obtain the independent air arm that it asked for. Whereas all the other navies in the thirties concluded that naval operations, submarine, surface or in the air, should be commanded independently. For Göring and his entourage, it was indispensable to create an autonomous air force, with the general formation being the most important element with the specialisation in land and naval missions coming second. The air units that remained attached to the navy were confined to scout missions or tactical interventions within naval engagements. This explains why the German Navy was greatly lacking in fighter and reconnaissance planes and that these were sometimes used for secondary missions, notably those of transportation.

This is the reason why, when the war broke out in 1939, that the Seeluftstreitkraft only had outmoded planes, controlled and organised by the Luftwaffe. From November 1940, a cooperation was admittedly put into place with the Luftwaffe but the number and capacity of the planes available were very insufficient. Because of this, and in order to make up for the deficiency, Dönitz, in January 1941, managed to persuade general Jodl to convince Hitler to immediately subordinate to him a certain number of aircraft. With the creation of the new Atlantic air command (Fliegerführer Atlantik or FlFü Atlantik), the cooperation between the air force and the navy would increase with Generalleutnant Kessler taking command from January 1942. Aware of the weakness of the forces given to him, he immediately demanded more modern aircraft. He had, however, to wait until July to obtain 24 Junkers Ju-88C-6 and 4 four engine Heinkel He-177s. When, in January 1943, Dönitz took over the command of the navy, he managed once more to get Hitler to give him new aircraft.

Thanks to its long range reconnaissance planes, the FlFü Atlantik managed to give decisive assistance to the U-Boote Wolf Packs, notably in the search for convoys, an assistance which meant that fruitless patrols in empty waters could be avoided. With its long range Focke-Wulf FW Condor maritime reconnaissance aircraft, it even achieved spectacular successes in the destruction of Allied ships as in the case of July 11th, 1943 with the bombing of the *Duchess of York* and the *California*, with a displacement of more than 38,000 metric tons. However, the efforts of the Atlantic air command stalled due to the lack of aircraft and the fact that they were inadequately protected, counter attacked by fighters from the escorting aircraft carriers. An example is that of February 1944, when convoy OS69 was attacked, planes launched from the *Pursuer* shot down half of the attackers.

with the participation of those who would have to carry them out. Unlike the other armies, Dönitz was convinced of the value of what could be learned from experience. For him, the discussions that he had with his commanders, where they were apparently free to say what they wanted, were far from undermining his authority, but on the contrary, improved the efficiency of the submarines. For Dönitz, no strategy could succeed without a total understanding between the person who gave the orders and those who had to carry them out. During the Munich crisis, 25 submarines were positioned around Great Britain, with the mission of laying mines if the situation worsened. Upon their return, Dönitz rushed to ask the Commanders for their opinion on the validity of his orders that they only discovered whilst at sea. Faced with the unanimous criticism that revealed all the suicidal aspects of such a mission, Dönitz stated that he had noted these remarks and that he was prepared to change the orders to avoid pointless sacrifice.

Despite the initial success of the Wolf Pack tactic, it was never able to function at maximum capacity. Dönitz, aware of his lack of vessels and their weakness in observation, due to their low position in the water, tirelessly tried to obtain from the Luftwaffe air observation support. Indeed, a warship could not detect a convoy over 22 nautical miles away in good weather (roughly 35 km) whereas a plane could cover an area 10 times larger during the course of a mission. However, despite this obvious solution, he could not convince Göring, the man responsible for the resurgent German air force in the thirties, who replied once and for all that « *everything that flies belongs to us* ». Dönitz would have to do without.

Esprit de corps

Dönitz, from the outset of training, also wanted to instil his officers and crews with the esprit de corps of a service branch that he saw as being the spearhead of the German Navy. With this in mind, at the end of 1935, the initial problems behind them and the first contingents of officer cadets arriving at Kiel, Dönitz welcomed them with a formula that summed up his conception of the submarine branch. « *The Navy is the best of our armed forces. The submarine arm is the best of the Navy.* »

All distinguishing signs, whether the result of chance or imposed, that showed the difference between the submariner and his surface colleague, were encouraged, allowing an identity to be forged. In this way, the Commander's white cap, elegantly placed on the back of the head of the future « ace » Otto Kretschmer, was noticed by Dönitz who made it the distinctive mark of submarine commanders, even though the regulation dress stipulated the blue cap. The long beard too, worn by submariners upon their return from a mission, even if it was due much to the need to ration water (the reserves were very low on a Type VII, only 2,6 metric tons could be carried), as well as for hygienic reasons (the skin was better protected from the cold, damp, and diesel), distinguished the submarine personnel. It was the

above
A lieutenant's Schirmmütze (« Kaleunt »). U Boote commanders wore the white cap of the summer uniform in all seasons for its stylishness and as a sign of their belonging to the submarine arm.
(Militaria Magazine)

above
A sailor of U-57 with a particularly full beard, a perfect example of a submariner upon his return to dry land.
(P. de Romanovsky collection)

left
This unidentified « Kaleunt », wears the white crowned cap, symbolic of his arm and his office.
(P. de Romanovsky collection)

above right
After the fall of France in 1940, some submariners (including Kretschmer) discovered the cotton utility jackets abandoned in the ports by the BEF in France. These jackets, originally used for fatigues or training, modern in style, were functional and comfortable to wear. They soon became popular, to such an extent that the German Army produced its own version.
(P-M Rousseau collection)

sign of belonging to a world unto itself, the identifying sign of the U-Boot. The beard was also the symbol of a community of fate. In the same way as the absence of distinctive rank insignia, of no use on patrol where everybody knew the next man's role, it gave everybody the same appearance and lessened the visibility of the hierarchy of rank. Although rank did not disappear, it was obvious that every man belonged to the same group, sharing a common destiny, illustrating the saying « *one for all, and all for one* ». The variety of uniforms bore witness, in its way, to the peculiarity of the submarine branch. The crews, who were issued with regulation kit, helped themselves generously to captured stocks found in French bases in the summer of 1940. French navy blue and British khaki were therefore distributed, the latter being especially popular.

This community of fate (Schicksalgemeinschaft), the expression used by Dönitz to describe a U-Boot crew, where every man holds the fate of the others in his hands, explains why mistakes on the job, even if they were subject to general disapproval, were rarely punished in order to avoid adding further unease to a human error. Even when a man on watch duties fell asleep, Commander Lüth recommended « *not*

THE « ACE » KARL FRIEDRICH MERTEN

« *With the reintroduction of military service* (in 1935), *the crews brought with them a new wave of enthusiasm. They had nearly all served in the Hitler Youth, had experienced the tough environment of the National Labour Service, were very idealistic and carried out their tasks with joy. This contrasted with the old professional sailors of the Reichsmarine, for whom the limited possibilities of promotion had blunted their military ambitions and which often led to discipline problems* ».

Karl Friedrich Merten: *Nach Kompass: Lebenserinnerungen eines Seeoffiziers,* 1994.

making him feel at fault or constantly remind him of it. This man is a comrade and entirely part of our community. »

This community was also renowned for what one could liken to superstitions but which were, in fact, identifying symbols or rituals of belonging. If we look at the case of Commander Schultze, who was willingly superstitious, we notice that he managed to convince the helmsmen that the route traced by the navigator should always be dividable by seven. If by chance, a newly arrived sub-lieutenant said, « *steer 227* », the helmsman would reply with « *understood Sir, steer 224* ». Although this custom was originally superstitious in origin, the fact that it was used seems to be more in keeping with the logic of belonging initiated by Dönitz. It was because they were Schultze's crew and that they had faith in him that they carried out these odd habits without raising an eyebrow.

In the same way, the pair of women's tights, fished out of the sea and rolled into a ball, became a talisman to Prien's U-47, it was passed around the crew before an attack, sometimes quickly kissed, even by the officers. The fact that everyone participated in this ritual is revealing in itself. It was more than a magic talisman, the tights were, above all, the symbol of a tightly knit crew in its entirety, to which each man pays homage, a sign of both his belonging and that which renews it. To this we need to add the customs to which a commander, even if he was an « ace », could not allow himself to go against. Each commander had their own way of dealing with the demands of the crew without losing face. Erich Topp, the Commander of the « red devil » submarine, was faced with having to leave on Friday 13th, he resolved the problem by casting off the day before, and going to the other side of the dock before continuing the next day. When U-99 had to leave on October 13, 1940, the crew asked commander Kretschmer to drop anchor and to start the ship's log on the 14th, a demand that was backed up by Warrant Officer 2 Petersen, who had served under the same commander since 1937. In order to not appear as giving in to what looked like an order, Kretschmer refused, but found a problem with the engine at just the right moment. The time for casting off was put forward until the 14th, at 1.30 am.

above
The forward part of a submarine's thick hull under construction, two workers climb out of the future torpedo tube apertures.
(DR)

The training of the men and the machine

This esprit de corps was even stronger in that it focused around a boat that, for its crew, was not just another numbered hull in which the men were interchangeable ; they were, along with their commander, one of the bonds that made up the unit. The recruiting procedures for active service in the submarine arm is revealing. As with navies the world over, it was out of the question to deliver a turnkey arm, especially given that the missions it would have to undertake would need experienced professionals who had undergone intensive training and who were able to form one body with their boat and its unique peculiarities. The first to see this was obviously the Commander when he entered into the last stages of construction. Accompanied by his future chief engineer and sometimes his first watch officer, he began the process of Baubelehrung, or « construction knowledge ». This four to six week period allowed officers to familiarise themselves with the vessel, to talk with the builders about its abilities, suggest modifications and, above all, to get to know each other before going aboard.

This first period was followed by a second of equal importance during which the crew were

A submarine under construction is launched rearwards. One can see, on the slipway, the bow dive planes.
(P-M Rousseau collection)

help of its crew, the submarine was officially baptised and became part of the Kriegsmarine ; Each submariner received a small souvenir from the shipyard, a coffee mill or a photo album during the baptism ceremony, where local dignitaries fought the submarine veterans for the best places.

After its baptism, the boat began its tour of all the different institutions that were responsible for testing its strength and

invited to the shipyard. In this way, everyone took part in the finishing touches, even though the different propulsion systems were installed, those of the diesel pipes and exhaust valves were in the process of being installed and as no flooring had yet been added, it was possible to see what was ordinarily hidden from view, such as the cooling water pipes or those of the pumps. After being completed with the

below right
An embroidered breast eagle for the crossover double buttoned jacket (Überzieher) or thick sweater, also called the Collani after a known tailor.
(F. Bachmann collection)

below
The Weddigen flotilla at sea.
(DR)

the installation of the various necessary equipment. Upon reaching the port of Kiel, it underwent a week of different trials by the Submarine Test Commission, the UAK (Uboot-Abnahme-Kommando), made up of a chief mechanic, a construction officer and an engineer. Pressure tests were carried out in a specially made dock to see how the boat reacted to maximum anticipated depths (more often, submarines were simply filled with extremely high pressure air, this would escape from the boat via any passages in the hull), this was followed by the installation of the torpedo laun-

U-960 signalling to a target ship during an exercise. *(DR)*

ching controls and the first surface launches. Once these operations were completed, the submarine was sent to Gotenhafen for a week where it was subjected to the investigations of the Technical Trials Commission, the UAG (Uboot- Abnahmegruppe) made up in the same way as the previous commission but with the addition of an active officer, who examined all the installations during dive exercises, which in the case of deficient equipment, allowed for the boat to be sent back to the Dantzig arsenal to iron out any defects.

When these tests were completed, the submarine was attached to a training flotilla where, during a three-week period, it could undergo its first endurance trials, before going to Röhne, on the island of Bronholm, in order to test out its underwater detection system, tests that were carried out with the help of coastal defence ships. All sorts of exercises were undertaken to give crews an idea of what they would have to face during attacks in the Atlantic. The commander would, during the course of these exercises, stop certain machines or turn off the lights so that the crew could get used to manoeuvring in darkness as experience had proved that this could happen.

This sort of exercise was no doubt of great use to the crew of the future commander Werner. During his first dive in the Baltic, because of a technical incident with one of his ballast tank doors, Werner's submarine dived straight to the bottom and became stuck in the silt 142 metres below the surface at a 45° angle. In the darkness, and subjected to chlo-

below

On U-53, the crew of the 105 mm gun (later replaced by the 88 mm) practice firing. One can make out the gunner (Kanonier), the loader (Ladeschütze) and the layer (Richtschütze). The gun could fire 12 rounds per minute and had an effective range of 6,000 metres. It could revolve around 360° and a negative line of sight of 4° and a positive sight of 30°. *(DR)*

rine fumes that escaped from the battery compartments, the crew had to pass buckets of water to the rear in order to balance the submarine. It finally rose to the surface after 20 hours.

It was only once these trials had been completed that the boat could at last begin its tactical exercises. It was then placed at the disposition of the Combat Training Group, the AGRU-Front (Ausbildungsgruppe für Front U-boote), whose commissioners remained on board. In charge of testing everything, the latter were exclusively made up of veteran sub-

right
A practice « Eel » torpedo, painted red and white to aid observation and recovery. *(DR)*

above
The front cover of a booklet published in 1942 showing the plans of U-31.
(P-M Rousseau collection)

left
Admiral Arnauld de La Perrière began his distinguished submarine career on board U-35, the boat which sunk the highest number of Allied ships during the First World War with 224 ships sent to the bottom, constituting more than half a million metric tons. He was attached to Brest in 1940 and took over the command of the navy for Western France (Marinebefehlshaber West Frankreich) which controlled the sector from the Loire to Spain. He died in a plane crash in 1941. He is seen here wearing the « Pour le Mérite », the highest German decoration of the First World War which he won in October 1916.
(ECPAD)

previous page top
Specialist sleeve insignia of the anti aircraft gun chief or small vessels, for the summer uniform.
(F. Bachmann collection)

mariners. Outstanding specialists and technicians were associated with commanders and chief mechanics who had served operationally. This was the final test and particularly tough for the boat and its crew. During the fifteen days of this technical examination, which covered an entire area of the Baltic, attack exercises were sometimes very realistic, tiring and exhaustive, against simulated convoys made up of all types and ages of decommissioned merchant ships, escorted by destroyers, torpedo boats and other anti submarine vessels. The submarine's task was made even harder by the fact that the merchant ships, sailing one behind the other in zigzag formation, were protected by a flotilla of counter-torpedo boats that had taken part in this sort of exercise since the outbreak of war (and who knew what time the simulated attacks would take place), and fifty planes that controlled vast areas, signalling the presence of all submarines detected in the area. It was, therefore, very difficult to get through without being spotted. The exercise was more than just the study of how well they could launch torpedoes, the objective was above all, to see the way in which the submarines manoeuvred and counter attacked once they had been spotted.

After having passed through the Torpedo Test Section, TVA (Torpedoversuchsanstalt), that supervised the loading of the torpedoes and their placement in the tubes, the boat joined the tactical flotilla to continue its training. This time it was not a case of test firing exercise torpedoes, but live launches with torpedoes that carried 200 kg of recording devices, set so that they would pass underneath the target. During this tactical examination, only the launching calculations (aim), were given to the target ship, so that the hits could be later examined and the training of the submarine crew evaluated. The target ship indicated the hits with a light, showing where the ship had been hit. In the same way that hunters are armed, the prey had the means to defend itself.

In response to the submarine's torpedoes, were the depth charges, that although dropped fifty or a hundred metres away, could still violently shake a detected submarine.

Due to the realism of the training, there were regular accidents, sometimes with terrible consequences. Before the war, U-18, during a dive attack close to its target, was in collision with a torpedo boat and sank. At a depth of 105 metres, its crew assembled in the last two unaffected compartments at the rear whose air supply would only last 14 hours. Given the impossibility of bringing up a crane, an emergency evacuation was contemplated. However, because of the pressure on the seabed (1 kg per 10 metres), no man was saved, the only men to escape were the five men thrown overboard from the deck at the time of the colli-

above

A submarine has been placed on dry land and pulled up onto the slipway before being led on rails to a concrete bunker where it will be careened and repaired. *(DR)*

below

True to the tradition of towns adopting vessels, U-960 was adopted by the town of Potsdam when it entered service. Major Wassner, of the Heer, is in charge here of the ceremony which is paced under the patronage of the Führer. On the left of his portrait can be seen the KM flag and on the left, that of the NSDAP. *(P-M Rousseau collection)*

sion. Another incident took place during the fleet manoeuvres watched over by admiral Horthy, the Regent of Hungary, on June 17th, 1938. The Graf Spee, rammed and damaged the conning tower of U-35. With all these accidents, some wanted to equip submarines with red-orange lights for the dangerous night exercises, and stopping the short distance attacks that were at risk of collisions. However, these propositions were obstinately refused by Dönitz who was convinced that the reality of these exercises would protect the men against the more extreme dangers they would face in wartime operations. In total, 26 U-Boote and 602 men were lost during these months of training; none were due to enemy action.

Once these tactical exercises were completed, the submarine left for Kiel from where it

cast off for Wilhelmshaven to complete its weaponry. Upon returning to Kiel, it went back a final time to the pressurized dock and was loaded with its last contingent of weapons before setting off to its base on the French coast. However, on its way to France, it stopped at Drontheim (Norway) for an examination of its underwater listening and detection devices in bathymetric conditions that were different from

those of the Baltic. Upon arriving in Bergen, the exterior of the hull was examined once more, before its definitive departure to its base where it would pass through the Arsenal for the last time before becoming operational. In total, a U-Boot would have to wait between six and twelve months before becoming operational, a duration that despite the pressure of events, the General Staff prevented its reduction until the end. Apart from the risks of an insufficiently tested boat, this period allowed the crew to realise just how much they were dependent on each other.

left
« *A submarine is sunk here* ». In peace time, submarines were equipped with a distress buoy which could be launched from the submarine, allowing for telephone communication with the crew.** *(DR)*

above
Major Wassner on the conning tower of U-960. The town which adopted the U-Boot gave the commander a visitor's book containing not only all the councillors' telegrams of congratulation and best wishes, but also those of submarine colleagues and the drawings of the town's school children. *(Private Collection)*

left
Soldbuch (an individual booklet that a man kept on his person) and Wehrpass (Kriegsmarine registration booklet). *(Private Collection)*

right
The arrival of volunteers and conscripts into the submarine arm. *(P-M Rousseau collection)*

TRAINING THE MEN

Training the officers

Submarine officers, despite the process of recruitment, were a very mixed group if we examine them according to how they behaved at sea. At the opposite end of the excellent tacticians and leaders, was a very small number of bad officers who were incapable of going to war; the majority could be found somewhere between the two. On the other hand, on a social and geographical basis, the group was homogenous. These were men from northern Germany, with a crushing majority of protes-

During their basic training, the young officers-to-be went to Rügen Island before joining the naval school. Here they underwent particularly tough training. Here they are preparing a rifle shooting exercise.
(P-M Rousseau collection)

tants (85 %), from middle and upper class families. Nevertheless, there were also volunteers from Silesia (a region situated mostly in the south west of the defunct Poland and with its borders on the Czech province of Moravia. From 1939, it was attached in its entirety to the Reich). It would also appear that quite a lot of electro-technicians from the Protectorate of Bohemia and Moravia (provinces reputed for being on the cutting edge of industry and technique) were pointed towards the submarine arm.

Contrary to modern day recruitment methods, there were not any specific tests in order to join the Navy. The Navy remained attached to its old methods, consisting of writing a long letter explaining why you wanted to join. Most of the applicants, after having had their medical and being made aware of the regulations, then went to one of the training centres, of which there were three before war broke out : one at Kiel for the Baltic area, another at Wilhelmshaven for the North Sea and the third on Germany's largest island, that of Rügen, which specialised in the training of midshipmen.

Upon arrival, recruits were plunged into a particularly hard and austere environment. The selection process was merciless, if only to remain within the limits (at least until the beginning of the 1930s) imposed by the Treaty of Versailles (roughly 500 naval officers). The 124 men who graduated in 1926, were selected out of 6,000 (a ratio of 1 in 50). But even when the number of officers increased, the ratio stabilised at 1 in 25/30. A fair amount of applicants were rejected in the first two days as they were not capable of doing the required physical exercises. The aim of this particularly hard training was to found the basis of elementary techniques of survival and discipline necessary for serving in the armed

WHEN GERMANY NEEDED CREWS THAT WERE « PERFECTLY TRAINED IDEOLOGICALLY »

« On March 14th, the German newspaper, National Zeitung *from Essen, published an agreement which had been made between the High Command of the Kriegsmarine and the leadership of the Hitler Youth, citing that future seamen should be recruited from the ranks of the Navy branch of the Hitler Youth. It is particularly interesting to read the newspapers remarks :*
« The High Command of the Kriegsmarine and the leadership of the Hitler Youth have created, thanks to this agreement, all the conditions which will provide the Kriegsmarine with young recruits capable of facing the increased hardships of wartime service.
Within every profession in Great Germany, there is a strong enthusiasm for sailing and the Kriegsmarine. Now there is the opportunity to be of use through effective activity and to prepare oneself for service in the Kriegsmarine. Success is inevitable. »
Germany, therefore, needs more personnel. We did not know that the German Navy needed more men. Its surface warships don't come out of their burrows in the Bay of Heligoland and content themselves with parading behind protective minefields. The crews from the merchant navy, of no use from now on, should be more than enough to cover their recruitment needs unless... The truth is that Germany has had its U-Boot crews decimated. Among the personnel of his fleet who know the submariner's life is like the convict's, or rather the condemned man's, Admiral Raeder cannot find any more volunteers. He has to, therefore, knock at a new door and he believes that the Hitler Youth in their blind devotion to the Führer, seem to fit the bill perfectly for serving on submarines. The text of the agreement itself underlines very well what the role of these young sailors is, as it gives credit to their "ideological style"
The German High Command has long called upon the Hitler Youth for its submarine crews. The English have seen proof of this in the survivors they have picked up from submarines they have sunk. The men were all young, most were smooth cheeked and seemed to be physically ill prepared for the difficult job that was theirs. They were, however, perfectly trained ideologically...
As for the inevitable successes mentioned in the remarks made by the Essen national socialist newspaper, it no doubt is in reference to the brilliant scuttling of the Graf Spee, *the internment of its crew and the cruel losses of the submarine fleet. »*

An extract from the Information bulletin of the French Navy, *N° 23, April 1st, 1940, page 14*

forces. This method was the same for all men, from the sailor to the officer, and for all service branches, be it on the surface or under water.

Upon admission, the young men left for Stralsund, then Dänholm, the island where all things maritime were taught. This lasted for three months in an extremely cold climate (-40°) and where the discipline was hard. They were issued with their uniforms, two in blue cloth, a white summer uniform, utilities for exercises, a bad weather suit, protective grey leather clothing, a rifle and gas mask. After being woken at 6 am, the recruits would parade at 7 am. The day would begin with two hours of exercise in the place known as « The valley of death » which was spread between two areas of high ground, every man had to climb both

above
The port of Stralsund.
(P-M Rousseau collection)

below
A model 1935 steel helmet (in its 1935-1940 manufacture) with decals representing the eagle of armed forces (Wehrmacht) tinted in gold (specific colour of the Kriegsmarine). It remained until August 1943.
(P-M Rousseau collection)

hills, those who could not were definitively eliminated. The exercise was made even more arduous on occasion as the men had to wear their polar uniform ; this consisted of wearing all their uniforms (the two blue uniforms, the grey leather clothing, wool hat, greatcoat, gloves, helmet, backpack and other accessories), the young men were then led into an over heated room where they had to do 20 push ups. It was only at 6 pm that the day was finally over, after dinner with their instructor officers, they were free for two hours. At 10 pm, everyone went to their bunks for a night which was often interrupted by an inspection carried out by the man in charge of the barrack-room.

The aim of all these exercises was obviously to toughen up the applicants and to check on how determined they were to join Naval

Military basic training (discipline, endurance exercises, preparation of infantry combat...), was similar to that of other arms. It was an indispensable prelude to specific Kriegsmarine training.
(P-M Rousseau collection)

Officers Corps. The physical tests were only one aspect. Added to this were the tests aimed at calculating reflexes, which sometimes bordered on the absurd. Wolfgang Ott, in his 1956 novel, « Sharks and Little Fish », talks of a particularly tough test. « *There was a person who read out a list of numbers as quickly as he could. Each time he said an even number, I had to raise my left arm, and the right arm if it was an odd number. If a number could be divided by three, I had to stamp my right foot on the ground. With a prime number I had to shake my head. This is no joke, Sirs, it was a torture house* ». Finally, the last test, the Mutprobe, or test of courage, consisted of lifting an iron bar through which was passed a painful electric current. Even though these methods were partly irrational, they revealed themselves to be particularly efficient and contributed to the bonding of new recruits. Those that managed to come through these tests rarely failed later on, less than 5 % of the 1934 Crew.

After a year of such training, they took part of the midshipman's exam at Kiel. A medical examination to test the applicants' reflexes followed these exams. This stage over, the trainees could at last get to grips with the sea, joining the port where they would undergo three months of training aboard one of the three school sailing ships : the *Gorch Fock*, *Albert Leo Schlageter* and the *Horst Wessel*, each with a displacement of 1,000 metric tons. Once aboard, the men were split into two watches, port and starboard. They were assigned hammocks and a personal locker, 50 cm high,

above
Cadets learn the basic maritime skills as they play at being top man on the topsails of the school ships. (Horst Wessel seen here) *(P-M Rousseau collection)*

below
Woven breast eagle for the white summer overblouse (Bluse). *(PC)*

wide and deep. The rigor and rhythm was the same as at Stralsund, with reveille at 6 am, followed by the folding up of hammocks in a very tight roll, and getting dressed in the exercise uniform for an inspection on the deck. For washing purposes, basins were filled with freezing water in the fresh air at 5 am, which often meant that the ice had to be broken before being able to wash. The men had to wait several weeks before being allowed, once dressed,

left
The monument raised in honour of submariners at Kiel. *(DR)*

Opposite
Flensburg-Mürwick Naval School : the first boats come out. *(P-M Rousseau Collection*

following page
The school ship *Niobé*. Its capsizing in 1932 prompted the design of a new class of sailing ship, the *Gorch Fock* and *Albert-Leo Schlageter*, which amongst other things, had an initial stability and a righting lever curve which meant that the ship could be righted even if she heeled over. *(DR)*

into the washroom. Those who risked turning up in underwear, were made to climb the main mast barehanded, to develop their sense of touch in order to understand their use rapidly.

The apprenticeship was entirely based on the necessity to develop the maritime senses of the young midshipmen who began their apprenticeship by mastering the different knots, splicing, towing a cutter, using a compass, coastal navigation, hours spent in the swimming school (using oars in the lifeboats) and the hard trade of the topman, in masts of up to 40 metres high. To be a good sailor also meant keeping the ship spick and span ; with this in mind, sailing school ships were models of cleanliness, all metallic parts were regularly polished so that they shined like gold. The deck was scoured several times a week with sandstone and water. There was nothing bet

below

Two of the German Navy school ships, the *Horst Wessel* and the *Gorch Fock*, photographed in 1940 at Kiel. The *Horst Wessel* was built by the Blohm and Voss naval shipyards at Hamburg. It was taken by the Americans in 1945 and renamed the *Eagle*, it still sails to this day as a training ship for the US Coast Guards.

(P-M Rousseau collection)

Schulschiff "Niobe" unter Segel.
Nach dem Original von Admiral Wölfram.

ter than physical exercise to nip complaints in the bud ; sails were unfurled and folded, anchors weighed and dropped with the windlass, all thanks to muscle power.

Moving the ship in port became a real tour de force. After having placed a lifeboat in the water, loaded with a one ton anchor at its stern, the men would row for one hundred metres in the direction of the new anchorage, drop

anchor and rejoin the ship, the anchor secu-
ring the ship would be weighed, and the ship
led towards the position of the first anchor
with the help of a capstan. At the end of this
term, the midshipmen were now called cadets
and could wear the distinctive star of their
rank, surrounded with gold cable stitch, on
their sleeve.

They now finally joined, for a new term, a
cruiser school ship, the *Schleswig-Holstein* or
its sister ship, the *Schlesien*. Put into service
during the First World War, these ships, with
four 280 mm guns, lent themselves perfectly
to extremely tough training where any mistake
resulted in a particularly harsh punishment. Woe
betide the man who, during changeover exercises, tore an item of clothing, the resulting punishment was to lift up the heavy rowing boats whose ropes (with hoists and pulleys), due to their
length and thickness, caused blisters.

On a more serious note, the first gunnery
exercises began using blank charges, then with
reduced charges for fairly distant targets and

above
**The *Schlesien* (*Deutschland*
class), built by the Schichau
shipyards and launched
in 1906.**
(P-M Rousseau collection)

finally with carefully chosen munitions. In the
evening, the cadets would have to fill in their
logbooks with all the details of their service,
this was often done in the heads or in the hold
as there was not any lighting in the sleeping
quarters.

above
**A raised design of a ship
of the line, probably the
Schleswig-Holstein or its sister
ship, the *Schlesien*.**
(P-M Rousseau collection)

left
**Even though motors could save
energy, hauling in a ship using
the capstan was still one of the
instructors' favourite exercises.**
(P-M Rousseau collection)

Although treated like sailors during the course of all this training, at the end of this pha-
se, they took an exam, that if they passed, allowed them to gain the rank of Fähnrich zur See,
the first rank of officer in the German Navy.
They could then join the naval school at Mürwick, nicknamed the « Castle », just outside
Flensburg. After having integrated the school,
they continued, for a year, theoretical training
that remained coupled with the learning of
practical knowledge. In a continuation of their
cadet training, the aim was above all to tou-

ghen up their maritime senses. Exercises included sailing, motor boats, exercises for coming alongside and mooring plus several voyages on large 1,000 ton steam ships.

The theoretical teaching, which focused on torpedo launching and the firing of large guns, whilst intensive (in 1936, there were 46 hours of instruction in the week), remained very generalised. This was due to the diversity of the types of ships and new weaponry, those in charge of training believed that a detailed teaching of all the weapons was attempting the impossible. On the other hand, efforts were made to develop the men's leadership qualities, it

above
Engineer pupils at the Flensburg-Mürwick naval school. The man on the right wears the cogwheel identifying him as belonging to the « engine » branch.
(ECPAD DAM 09 L35)

left
« Baptism certificate », awarded in the name of Neptune, to a sailor of the *Schlesien* in 1937 for having crossed the equator.
(P-M Rousseau collection)

below
A view of the « castle », the naval school of Flensburg-Mürwick.
(P-M Rousseau collection)

was therefore, not surprising that they read Erich-Maria Remarque's « All Quiet on the Western Front », or that they studied the mutinies of 1918. In order to lead men one had to know them and this was the reason why the sub lieutenants were given all the jobs to do on a submarine before being made watch officer.

At the end of these twelve months, they took the main officer's exam (Offiziershauptprüfung), which, once obtained, finally allowed them access to the high seas aboard a cruiser school, where, at the end of the cruise, they were promoted to the full status of Oberfänhrich zur See — the heritage of Prussian regiments — (this rank is the equivalent of Lieutenant Junior in the Royal Navy, midway between that of midshipman and acting sub

lieutenant). The duration of the training period, for many midshipmen, decreased in the second half of the 1930s and even more so in the 1940s.

When Hitler gained power, the duration of the training period went from 54 months in 1930, to 42 in 1933, 36 in 1934 and only 30 in 1938. Once the clauses of the Treaty of Versailles had been lifted, having such a stringent selection process could no longer be justified. Germany needed to rebuild large and powerful armed forces. The Navy was included in this process, especially as its plan for reconstruction, Plan Z, put together by the Chief of the General Staff for the German Navy, Admiral

left
Flensburg-Mürwick. This future officer wears on his white shirt the two rank stripes with a trade insignia above (cog wheel) which identify him as a Maschinen Obergefreiter (able seaman). He also wears the insignia of searchlight technician, an inherent component of coastal artillery training, an essential speciality which opened the door to technical specialities concerning the engines.
His companion wears the insignia of a petty officer (cog wheel with red anchor) and the red cogwheel above a stripe as a trade insignia, signifying that he has had the basic training of an electro technician.
(ECPAD/DAM 08 L14)

right
At the school of Neustadt-in-Holstein in 1939-1940, the future naval officers catch up on the latest news.
(P-M Rousseau collection)

below
The future members of U-Boote crews undergo anti aircraft gunnery training. The men on the central anti aircraft gun are on a mobile platform moved by machinery underneath. This allowed the men to get used to the movements of the submarine and to aim in an almost automatic fashion at a fast moving target.
(P-M Rousseau collection)

Raeder in 1938, demanded an officer corps much bigger than the tiny number of 500. However, whereas the duration of the round the world cruise was sacrificed, or part of the theoretical lessons, the experience of commanding remained a priority. In December 1939, for example, cadets spent three months in basic training, three months aboard the *Gorch Fock*, then six months aboard minesweepers or patrol boats, or submarines, then five months of lessons at « The Castle ». At the end of these 17 months they were operational.

Those who opted for the submarine arm, joined the « Dönitz Free Corps », which had two main motivations, patriotic enthusiasm and promotion, as the branch allowed men to rapidly obtain the post of commander and to shine. They then joined the submarine school at Neustadt-in-Holstein for nine months, followed by five months at torpedo school. After these

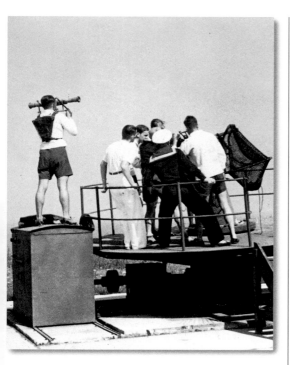

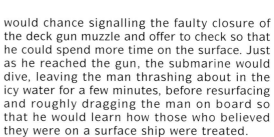

left
Recruits training to calculate the target distance using small optical range finders, devices which could not be used on the open sea when a plane dived towards them. Faced with a plane approaching at a speed nearing 100 metres per second, aiming had to be done immediately by guesswork. The exercises carried out here were, therefore, used to train men at judging distances rather than learning to use a range finder in a combat situation. *(P-M Rousseau coll.)*

right
The sextant was used to measure the angular distance of a star with the horizon. This model was part of a Kriegsmarine crew's equipment. *(P-M Rousseau coll.)*

below left
The Marine-Studienrat (instructor of naval studies) Gelembus gives a lesson (1941) at the naval school of Flensburg- Mürwick. *(AK)*

above
A trade insignia (that of a helmsman), yellow for the blue cloth uniforms, was woven with blue thread for the white uniforms. *(F. Bachmann collection)*

long and hard years of study, they finally embarked, two or three at a time, on a submarine for their first mission in a combat zone, the mission being the end of their apprenticeship. Their last instructor was, therefore, their commander, and although the latter could be full of benevolence, the realities of combat could sometimes make the presence of these young midshipmen badly timed.

The first contact could sometimes be a little cold, as related by the 18-year-old Voolkmar König, when he was met by Otto Kretschmer. After being abruptly questioned about what he believed he knew about the subject of submarines, and managing to reply with what the midshipmen's training school had taught him, he received the peremptory

reply : « *Well then, I suppose that you are going to tell me how to wage war during your first voyage. I'll soon make you forget those ideas.* » Kretschmer had himself received a frosty welcome from his own commander.

During training in the Baltic, the continuous exercises preventing the young officer from having time to smoke a cigar in peace, he

would chance signalling the faulty closure of the deck gun muzzle and offer to check so that he could spend more time on the surface. Just as he reached the gun, the submarine would dive, leaving the man thrashing about in the icy water for a few minutes, before resurfacing and roughly dragging the man on board so that he would learn how those who believed they were on a surface ship were treated.

Once aboard, the Commander was there to remind these beginners that they did not amount to much and that they had three weeks in which to get used to things, a duration which corresponded to the entry into the combat zone. On the submarine, they were directly attached to a member of the crew and they received their orders from the Commander and Watch Officer. They learned quickly how to move around the confined space and where every pipe came from, where it went and what it was for. They studied the charts, went on watch on the deck and even took over from Watch Officers or Petty Officers during calm periods. If the rank held was that of Oberfähnrich, he could be in charge of a watch and take on the role of an officer. Their life, however, was hard and they were shouted at by veterans whenever the inevitable mistake was made. The men of the crew would make them crawl under the steel flooring or make them

The German patrol boat TF 17-11. Cadets spent six months on minesweepers or patrol boats. *(P-M Rousseau collection)*

clean the holds so they would get to know every inch of the ship.

The tutors were Chief Petty Officers who carried out the same every day essential tasks as the officers. Destined to lead men, they had to know how the latter lived. Taking it in turns, they were sent to the various posts, with the crew, the Leading Seamen and the Petty Officers, they also took it in turns to eat in the

KRETSCHMER'S STANDING ORDERS FOR ACHIEVING PERMANENT EFFICIENCY:

« I — A faultless alert system is of the utmost importance for any submarine operation. During raids at sea, the first condition indispensable for success is meticulous organisation. A weakness in the system of organisation could mean the destruction of the submarine and the death of its crew.

II — Aviation plays a greater and greater role in the enemy's tactics in the fight against submarines. It represents a deadly danger for all submarines on the surface. The lookouts have, therefore, the task of not only looking for any surface movement but also to observe the sky vigilantly. It is necessary for the lookouts to set off the air alert early enough to give us enough time to dive to a depth of 20 metres, safe from any detection or bombardment.

III — Isolated ships not sailing under a neutral flag or that of the Red Cross should, if they appear to belong to the enemy, be sunk with the gun in order to save the torpedoes for escorted targets. If it is absolutely impossible to destroy them with the gun, torpedoing will of course be authorised.

IV — If the boat is not exposed to un-necessary danger, and if there is enough time, the survivors should be helped as we would expect to be helped by the enemy if U-99 was sunk.

V — Only attack convoys in the daytime if it is impossible to wait for nightfall. Daytime attacks against convoys mean a careful assessment of the risks and should only be carried out after all the factors have been considered. In particular, the probable successes should be weighed up to see if they are worth taking such risks.

VI — If the circumstances are normal, U-99 will shadow convoys in the daytime, and it will only place itself in an attack position at nightfall. If there is moonlight, the submarine will have to moor fore and aft to attack from the dark side of the convoy. The merchant ships will be silhouettes against the light, whilst our silhouette, low in the water will be almost impossible to see.

VII — If there is little or no moon, U-99 will always attack from the side the wind is blowing from. The enemy lookouts having to face the wind, often with rain and spray in their faces, will always be less efficient than those observing with the wind at their backs.

VIII — Spreads of torpedoes launched from far away do not offer any guarantee of success and represent a considerable waste. U-99 will act according to my principle which means that it should not be necessary to launch more than one torpedo per ship.

IX — The rule above necessarily means that we have to open fire from a short distance. However, this is not possible until the escorts defensive barrage has been passed, sometimes even after having placed ourselves in the lines of merchant ships.

X — The attack launched in these conditions, and at night, we should never dive under any account, except in the case of extreme danger. As a general rule, I am the only one who will give the order to dive. These instructions are based on the certitude that a submarine on the surface can manoeuvre at high speed to avoid danger and that it can counter attack, if necessary, thanks to its torpedoes and its rapidity. If we are pursued, one must not forget that when the submarine is submerged, it becomes slow and is then at the mercy of the hunter.

XI — Remind yourselves that, at night and on the surface, you will see a ship faster than it will see you. The counter torpedo boats and other submarine hunters will easily detect you thanks to their ASDIC as soon as you dive. On the other hand, they will not pick up your presence if you move away on the surface.

XII — U-99 will dive every day for two hours just before dawn, for two reasons. Firstly, we will avoid the risk of hastening towards enemy ships that would have been hidden by the darkness. Next, we will use our hydrophones for listening to enemy movement. Finally, the crew will, during this interval, be able to relax, wash and have their breakfast in peace. »

officers' mess. If they performed well, their commander would recommend them for officers' training lessons, before returning as a Second Watch Officer. In certain cases, a trainee commander (Kommandantenschüler), sometimes called Konfirmand (Confirmed), came back on board for a patrol. This was an officer who had proved himself in training but who had not yet been confronted with the reality of a patrol and his mission of Watch Officer. He could in this way gain experience thanks to the veterans of the crew.

At the end of this first sea training course, the question arose as to what to do with the midshipmen. Should they be sent on a mission to perfect their knowledge of the job, or remain in Germany to undergo training necessary to become a Watch Officer? Even though the lack of personnel became increasingly alarming during the course of the war, they had to perfect their training, at least until 1942. They remained for a six-month period to learn about the new torpedoes and the tactics relating to them, take the Radio Officer's exam and practice the different secret codes and signals. The end of this study period was crowned with a term at the Baltic navigation school where they carried out coming along side manoeuvres, underwater navigation exercises, simulated attacks and reconnaissance; they would then begin a week of theoretical lessons.

At the end of this term, they became Zweite Wachoffizier (Second Watch Officer), then Erst Wachoffizier (First Watch Officer), before being selected to command a submarine. In reality, Watch Officers could rapidly be placed observe the sea, its waves and even sunrise, followed by the appearance of a steamer and a convoy. These simulated exercises were completed by a course of practical training at Dantzig where the future commander multiplied, in a very short space of time, night and day attacks which tested his resistance to sleep deprivation. At the end of this final exam, the new commander could be called on to replace one of his colleagues at the Front, become himself an instructor at the submarine school or take command of a new boat from a shipyard of his choice. Although the first two years

« Beautiful Danzig »
(P-M. Rousseau collection)

in command of a ship, certain commanders did not hesitate in putting them in charge during certain exercises so that they could be replaced if needed.

To attain the command of a submarine, the Watch Officer went to Neustadt-in-Holstein where he underwent exercises on a simulator F (Führungsgerat : command machine), which saved on costly exercises. The pupil commander took up position in a conning tower which was the exact replica of that of a submarine and which had the same instruments. When looking through the periscope, he could

right
One of the two future dive plane men undergoing training. In front of him are the depth manometers and the pendulum which gave the boat's trim, allowing it to be corrected if necessary. Behind him, the chief mechanic keeps an eye on the depth. *(DR)*

below
A Steuermann shoulder strap (1st master helmsman).
(F. Bachmann collection)

of the war allowed this training and rigorous selection process to be carried out, the situation became more delicate to handle in the final two years. The General Staff did not hesitate in taking men from the reserve, men who had commanded with distinction mineswee-

A Torpedomechaniker shoulder strap (1st master torpedo man).

A Stabs obermaschinist shoulder strap (principal master of engines)

HOW TO LEAD MEN ON BOARD A SUBMARINE BY WOLFGANG LÜTH

« *The commander has the duty to make sure that the attitude of good soldiers prevails on his boat and that the opinion of bad soldiers has no value. As a comparison, he has to act on board like a gardener who pulls up weeds and looks after the good plants. This is not really difficult as we mostly have young sailors on board who only wish to do well. There is the advantage that the men have all learnt a trade, they must not be considered as half educated men who hardly ever went to high school or who had been thrown out of lessons or lacking in intelligence.*

If one of them behaved arrogantly towards a superior or had done something else which would have normally resulted in three days punishment, I did not give him the three days but made him "sleep rough". He would sleep on the deck without either a mattress or a blanket and as that was uncomfortable it was more effective than giving him three days punishment, which, furthermore, would have been written down in his pay book.

The ban on smoking constituted another severe punishment.

Three days of not being able to "shuffle the cards" worked miracles with the card players. During a cruise, the supplies having dropped inordinately, a "crafty type" had squirreled away his own supply, showing contempt for any spirit of comradeship and in such quantities, that severe measures were called for. On board a submarine it is impossible to lock up a sailor. On land, any court, even civil, would have severely punished him and sent him to prison. I solved it my way. I punished him with fifteen days of "banishment" in the way that had previously existed for cadets. No one was allowed to talk to him and during the entire period he slept on a board. In this way, the case was resolved and nobody spoke any more of it. Comradeship had been re-established. This man later became one of the best submariners, always ready for action.

It goes without saying that, on board, a commander must be available for his men at any time. I consider it absurd to keep one's distance. The men will then forget, out of fear, to report any happenings or important events.

Being a lookout is particularly important. It is more a question of character than good eyesight. During my patrols in all theatres of operations and with all types of submarines, we have seen more than 1,000 aircraft, but we have been bombed only three times. Even at night the lookout has spotted planes and in both cases heard them in time. I do, however, allow the men on watch to talk and smoke. I know that the staff at the base do not like that and that they have issued orders banning these practices. The men on watch on the bridge must have basic rules. But, it seems difficult to imagine them on watch for four hours without saying the slightest thing, especially when it is a patrol lasting several months. If they are careful I also let them squat down with their backs against each other, chatting about this and that as they look through their binoculars. Normally, alcohol is forbidden on patrols against the enemy. However, the men are grateful when they are allowed to drink from the

above
Wolfgang Lüth with the Knights Cross of the Iron Cross, awarded on October 24th, 1940. To this was added the oak leaves on 17th November, 1942 and the swords and diamonds on August 9th (or the 11th), 1943.
(ECPAD)

above
U-43, where Lüth was, for a while, the « Kaleunt ».
(DR)

bottle from time to time. For example, when a boat has been sunk, for a birthday or even when a sailor has been soaked when working on the deck. »

Wolfgang Lüth was very close to his men. He felt and thought like them and knew their weaknesses as well as their qualities. Lüth even wrote them standard letters from which they could choose what suited them when, upon returning to base, they wanted to write to their parents or sweethearts. He thought that the men would rather not write given the amount of things to be kept secret.

Everyday life was organised perfectly. Lüth said that the submarine had to be a second homeland for the men. However, not everything needed such an organisation. Time to rest was particularly necessary. It was generally admitted that rest and sleep was sacred to the submariner. The rhythm of his normal life had to be preserved. The change from day to night was not perceptible in itself and had to made visible or sensed in some way. The lights were dimmed for supper, and when the watch was changed at 20.00 hrs, the radio played the evening concerts from 19.30 to 20.30 hrs.

Sundays also had to be emphasized.
It would begin with a concert of records, beginning with, *I like staying in bed until 10 o'clock on a Sunday* and the evening concert would end with a suitable record such as, *Abenlied by the Pierrots of Regensburg cathedral.*

« *Thinking up the menus is an important and difficult job. I therefore let each post make up the different menus. I have to keep a tighter control on them when the patrol is prolonged so that the nice things are not eaten first. The bread is cooked on board. It had been a difficult job one day when the oven was playing up. We got round it by setting up a bakery contest. Four men, bakers by profession, had to bake bread one after the other. Each loaf that came out of the oven was given great publicity, as much as if not even more than for the elections of the Chamber of Deputies — by the radio or the log book. After that we really had decent bread.*

There are physical ailments which in no way prevent a man from being a good submariner. Many submariners have been declared as being unfit for service; they were no doubt, according to the rules, and for which no man wanted to take the responsibility of putting them in a crew and facing the enemy, even though they would have been fine. However, with so many soldiers risking their lives, others should, in the same way, risk their health in a severe war.

When we regain port, I make sure that the men buy as much as possible for their families and that they spend their money wisely. They must be given the opportunity to party at the base without any limits, simply because if they don't they will go astray to other bases.

There are, however, things that cannot be allowed. I had a watch officer who undressed to sleep on his bunk. At night he never arrived at his post without first having got dressed meticulously and with difficulty. He never forgot to come without his waterproofs. His personal well being was that important to him before he got to his combat post. He never drank coffee because he was a hypochondriac and he thought he had a problem with his stomach.

Instead he drank a glass of milk. I forbade this because we don't have a cow on board and we didn't have much milk. As well as this there were things that he didn't eat and at each meal he asked for a special dish. The crew soon got wind of this and decried the officers' mess, even before the commander had noticed anything.

In the mess the meals are taken together, and taken properly; white bed sheets (or at least relatively white) are used as table cloths. The daily card game should not be forgotten; it can be nice to talk together about books or literature.

The radio man is one of the most important men on board. He notices the torpedo boat before anyone realises what is going on. I forbid him to signal to me the presence of the torpedo boat and its movements out loud. Any information is passed to me by the orderly, a man chosen for his calmness who murmurs the information to me. The word "torpedo boat" is struck off from our vocabulary, we say "little boat" so that inexperienced men do not worry unduly.

We have to struggle to make men who are not on watch, go to their bunks and sleep. We have to make sure that they breath through their potassium filters so that the air is purified and oxygen saved. This naturally applied to officers who are not on watch, precisely because it is uncomfortable.

When all the preparations are made, it is good for the commander to go to his bunk as well. This makes the crew happy who think that "things are only half bad".

The organisation of leisure time is important, especially for feast days, and bank holidays merit particular attention. In the period of Advent, candles are lit in every post and garlands of paper hung up. These were made out of rolled up hand wipes and toilet paper, painted in green. For a fortnight, Christmas cakes are made and each man can eat as if he were at home.

Skat, chess and singing contests are fun. Each man sings into the microphone and the crew gives marks just like at school. The first prize consists of being spared a watch which is taken over by the commander. The sailor who obtains the second place either starts the diesels if he belongs to the deck specialists, or is authorised

above
Korvettenkäpitan Lüth back at base. Note the man on his right and opposite him, a leading seaman or a sailor, hanging on his every word in a communion which commander Lüth made an art of command. *(DR)*

above
Senior petty officer's and midshipmen's issue model blue cloth Schirmmütze.
(Militaria Magazine)

above
The insignia of the 1st U-Flotille, ex-Flotille Weddigen in peace time. Originally based at Kiel, it was only moved to Brest in June 1941.
(P. de Romanovsky collection)

to steer the boat in the place of the commander if he is a mechanic or driver. I am happy with any passionate debate that encourages word play. During long patrols, the strangest things can become object of discussion:

Do cows give more milk when listening to the radio?... or even... are the holes in cheese made by compressed air........or furthermore, the affirmation that storms at sea did not have thunder.

Each patrol comprises situations that cannot be mastered by orders or by obedience based on rigid principle.

After a particularly long stay in the arsenal, my crew was made up of more than one third of new men, notably amongst the officers and petty officers. The first boat that we came across during the patrol was a big one and was steaming at full speed. Only at night did we manage to get into a position to launch, and I said to the first watch officer, for whom it was the first patrol:

"You will launch the first torpedo towards the foremast and the second, calmly towards the mizzenmast."

The navy might no longer call these masts (fore and aft) by the names used in the age of the sailing ship. The WO1, keen to show his learning and very sure of himself said, but in too quiet a voice:

"Torpedo n° 1, fire"

in a way that the launch chief could not hear in the conning tower. It also seemed to me to be too quiet and I said to him: "For the second launch, you'll have to give the order louder."

This he did. However, the launch chief had not taken the off the safety catch for the launch and the second torpedo did not come out either. He was new on board, as was the petty officer second class mechanic, so that the information over the loudhailer did not happen in the same conditions as previously.

I immediately changed the other tubes and gave the order to fire on the steamer myself. However, the distance had become too short. No sooner had the "eels" been launched than we were spotted by the steamer which was turning towards us. We were in danger of being rammed, whilst the torpedoes were going to miss their target. I wanted to turn fully to port and I ordered:

"Full to port. Starboard engine full speed ahead, port engine full astern." But the new helmsman should have first placed the rudder to starboard. I first had to correct him, and the U-Boot thus turned only very slowly. On the other hand, the old petty officer second class mechanic had put the port diesel "full astern" and he thought that the new starboard diesel chief had fully turned as this one was "full speed ahead" He rushed over to it and placed the starboard diesel on "reverse".

So there I was with the two diesels "full astern" and the rudder set in the wrong position. With God's help everything worked out and we were not rammed. We chased the steamer which steamed at full speed and whose speed was one knot more than ours. I had, therefore, to admit that it was going to get away and that we had missed our chance. I could have cried. I didn't cry and I laughed. You should never give an impression of weakness to your men, nor show your nerves. »

Training the crews

The crews were formed on two submarine training flotillas, that of Pillau (renamed 21 U-Flotille on June 1st, 1940) and that based at Gotenhafen (renamed 27 U-Flotille in July 1940). They comprised around 36 boats which were especially destined for the training of the future submarine crews. This training was carried out on Type II submarines weighing 300 metric tons, which were unusable on the Front due to their slow speed and limited range. Being smaller, the crew lived in cramped conditions in the forward compartment. Duties were more tiring as there was less crew for the same tasks. The officers and crew also shared their time between hours of being on duty and hours of rest; during the periods of rest they had to set the torpedoes and maintain interior duty. The training programme was particularly accelerated with theoretical lessons given on land in special classes and with practical lessons given on board by permanent crews, reduced

pers and patrol boats. 179 reserve officers were, in this way, attached to the submarine branch between 1943 and 1945. This proportion, however, remained lower than that of the other services as it was 20 % in July 1942 compared to 35 % for the infantry, and 50 % for the Luftwaffe and in motorised divisions. The General Staff also took petty officers to be used as commanders. These, however, were few, with only 35 petty officers becoming officers during the course of the war. Faced with the need for officers, each naval command had, from 1944, to give 0.5 % of its personnel to the submarine arm.

The importance given to the U-Boote from 1944 is also illustrated by the replacement of those in charge of the Naval College by young U-Boote commanders. When the « ace » Wolfgang Lüth took over the command of this college on August 30th, all he could do was note the difficulty in carrying out the mission he had been given. Indeed, in the spring of 1944, the level of the cadets had reached its lowest point and there were some- times only one or two former watch officers that had combat experience. All of the others came from the surface fleet, or even the General Staff. Distraught, Lüth wrote that, « *they all lack the essential notions that only combat can teach, lightning reflexes, guessing the enemy's next move, the experience that allows one to know when to crash dive, or, on the contrary, to remain on the surface and fight with the deck gun* ».

Speeded up by events and in order to fulfil the demand, the former watch officers saw their training period reduced to two months of lessons before being immediately given a command. At the end of the war, it is estimated that out of the 100 commanders of the submarines in service, only a quarter were experienced men; of which only three had fought during the duration of the war.

above
Future crew members of U-96 taking the oath at the end of their final exam.
(P-M Rousseau collection)

right
Practical lessons on board.
A sailor takes part in repairs.
(DR)

above
The U-Boote war badge (U-Boot-Kriegsabzeichen). The creation of this badge was desired by Dönitz and agreed to by Raeder who instituted its creation on October 13th, 1939 on the eve of Kapitänleutnant Gunther Prien's historic exploit at Scapa Flow. It was awarded by the commander of the submarine fleet to all crew members who proved their worth in the face of the enemy during two or more patrols. The badges were made, until around 1942-43, in gilded bronze.
(Militaria Magazine)

to a minimum. It was these men who observed the cadets when they were at the posts they would later have to occupy. Each newly enlisted crew member finished his training in six months, this was then reduced to three, then two. For certain specialities, such as a radio operator or torpedo man, this could drop to five weeks. As the number of recruits increased, the time allocated to training decreased. In this way, out of the 15,000 cadets who passed through Gotenhafen between September 1942 and December 1943, some immediately joined operational submarines, others, made up of personnel with particular technical skills, had to replace submariners who were ill or employed elsewhere. The majority were attached to an operational reserve that received a rudimentary training but whose members had to be ready to board at any moment.

Nothing, however, replaced experience gained at sea, notably for those on watch duties, for whom the experience of watching the sea

and the horizon was irreplaceable. In any case, with the increase in losses, the newly built submarines had crews which were made up half of sailors who had taken part in combat missions (which entitled them to wear the U-boat war badge and the Iron Cross second class) and the other half of new recruits. In this way, in the spring of 1942, 25 % of new personnel had to be integrated each time U-71 set off, as there was no retraining programme that allowed crews to get used to new equipment. In reality, from 1941, certain crews were undertrained. U-570 cast off with a crew that was hastily assembled in two months, of whom half knew nothing of the submarine arm, including

above
A flotilla at port. 15,000 recruits passed through the Gotenhafen flotilla between September 1942 and December 1943. *(DR)*

right
A submarine war badge award certificate, awarded to Matrosenobergefreiten Lothar Trantow on January 23rd, 1941.
(P-M Rousseau collection)

below
A lookout on the bridge of U-9.
(P-M Rousseau collection)

the Commander. One therefore has to be careful with Dönitz's declarations that the submariners were the elite of the German Navy. Indeed, in 1940, this elite service branch was decimated by 40 % and meant that selection standards as well as training time were lowered.

Verleihungs-Urkunde

Auf Grund der Ermächtigung des Oberbefehlshabers der Kriegsmarine verleihe ich dem

Matrosenobergefreiten
(Dienstgrad)

Lothar T r a n t o w
(Name)

das

Ubootskriegsabzeichen 1939

Befehlsstelle, den   23. Januar   1941

The capture of U-570. Note the iridescent sea around the ship, condemned to surrender or a chase which it could not win. *(IWM)*

A postage stamp made in 1943, exulting the adventure of the submarines of the German state. *(E Bachmann collection)*

« *Alert ! Dive !* » The average time for a Type VII C to dive was 35 seconds.
(P-M Rousseau collection)

The submarine

Despite his wish to have a large fleet on the outbreak of war, indispensable for tightly covering the convoy routes, Dönitz could only rely on fifty submarines in August 1939 which meant that only twenty could be in the combat zone at the same time. Indeed, with any given number, only a third could be on patrol at the same time, the rest would be on their way to or from the zone, being repaired or on exercise.

Even if its costs were in no way comparable to a pocket battleship, the submarine was, ton for ton, more expensive, costing four million marks and needing 450,000 hours of work, this explains why some commanders were reluctant to launch their torpedoes against small ships of little value. It was senseless to risk detection and damage for a ship of insignificant value.

In the middle of the 1930s, the question of the choice of U-Boot Type was at the heart of Dönitz's problems, he openly favoured the construction of an ocean-going Type with a displacement of 750 to 1,500 metric tons, with an obvious preference for the Type VII (with a surface displacement of 600 metric tons) which was more able to face the North Atlantic storms than the 250 metric ton coastal submarines. Far from giving into the lure of the cruiser submarine (based on the French *Surcouf*), the U-Boote commander very quickly realised that his boats should in no way be affected by a logic that was forced upon other types of ship.

Submarines were in no way meant to fight other submarines and were, therefore, not affected by a tonnage or arms race. Differing from the French strategy of the dual role of protecting maritime routes and the coast, as well as attack combined with a surface squadron, the role of merchant shipping hunter assigned to them by Dönitz resulted in specific and exclusive requirements.

The Wolf Pack U-Boot had to be, above all, a boat capable of diving quickly. The Type VII could escape the ship hunting it in less than a minute, sometimes in half a minute after the alert had been given by the lookouts.

From 1943, due to improvements made to the diesels, the exhaust fumes were used to flush the water from the ballast tanks. The submarine could then dive in less than 30 seconds and quickly reach a depth of 40 metres. With the new risks brought about by the Allied developments in aviation, winning the « battle for seconds » (that is disappearing under water) had become a major priority. German engineers reduced the wide and flat hull that tended to make the U-Boote stick to the surface, thus allowing the reduction of the average time needed to dive to 35 seconds.

Apart from rapid diving, the boat was designed to resist a depth of more than 100 metres. In reality, many examples showed that its thick hull, made from special steel, could resist the pressure of more than 200 metres, and that 250 metres could be endured.

Leutnant zur See von Tiesenhausen's U-331 went down to 260 metres in November 1941 and U-331 would go to 266 metres, a depth

above
This non regulation, roughly made zinc badge (originally gilded), is a bit of an oddity. The lack of period documents does not allow us to know exactly who the badge was destined for. Frontreif can be translated as « Ripe for the Front ». This implies that this badge identified new Kriegsmarine personnel who had finished their training and were ready to begin their service on board a submarine. His design was used by U-295 and U-1003.
(Militaria Magazine)

top right
The thick hull of a submarine was made up of thick 18 to 35 mm steel sections, shaped and welded to frames that were spaced by approximately 80 cms (seen here in the photograph) and welded together.
(DR)

that would seem to be the maximum reached by a submarine that managed to reach the surface again. Beyond this depth, the submarine would be literally crushed by the pressure. In the case of damage to a part of the submarine, the area could be closed off by seven water tight compartments whose bulkheads could resist a pressure of 120 metres. However, with the improvement in Allied weapons, diving to a great depth was no longer a guarantee of escaping destruction. Getting away was more often the only chance of salvation.

It soon became unthinkable of fighting back seriously against attacks by aircraft. As they were only designed for attack or escaping, the U-Boote were of limited efficiency in surface warfare. Behind the bridge, the anti aircraft gun platform known as « the Winter Garden », was only equipped with twin 20 mm anti air-

left
Although the submarines' primary objective was merchant shipping, the destruction of Allied warships was a much envied exploit which the whole crew took pride in. It is, therefore, not surprising that one of the most famous submariners, Commander Prien, is remembered for his exploit at Scapa Flow and that the number one tube of Commander Von Tiesenhausen's U-331 which launched the torpedo that sank *HMS Barham* on November 25th, 1941, was the object of special attention.
(ECPAD)

right
The anti aircraft defence of U-333 was made up of two double 20 mm platforms and a four barrel gun of the same calibre (three of the barrels have been dismantled for maintenance).
(P-M Rousseau collection)

craft guns and a 37 mm canon (in 1944, certain boats were equipped with a heavier armament, such as U-441, which had eight 20 mm canons and one 37 mm canon. The 88 mm deck gun (or the 105) was finally deleted as it was not of much use. Once hit, the boat could find itself practically paralysed much faster than a surface vessel with similar damage. Indeed, if a shell hit it, diving was impossible and even a machine gun bullet in the exterior fuel tanks would mean it could be followed when under water. As well as this, the submarine had a very small reserve of floatability when under water and any reasonably important leak would be fatal.

It was even more vulnerable due to the lightness of its armour which made it a favourite target of Allied bombers. The hull's thickness of 25 mm did not offer much protection against 20 mm shells, like those that hit U-570, piercing the armour and devastating the control room. Finally, this fragility was increased by the extreme difficulty of carrying out repairs, when it was possible to make out the dama-

ged areas of the hull in a boat full of instruments. On the other hand, its small size allowed it to manoeuvre thanks to a small radius of gyration that meant it had several rapid options in the case of attack, allowing it to pull out quickly from dangerous negative buoyancy, which in times of war is an angle of 30°. Its small size also meant that it was a particularly discreet hunter, thanks to its low position in the water, although its conning tower was relatively high compared to foreign submarines, this was compensated by a deck that was practically at water level.

What it gained in size was lost in its autonomy compared to a larger vessel, capable of carrying more fuel thanks to its tanks which filled the last available spaces. The Type VII B, carried, in this way, 98 metric tons of diesel which gave it a range of 7,000 nautical miles (at an average speed of seven knots) which was barely enough for a theatre of operations the size of the Atlantic. Reaching the centre of the North Atlantic from the German Baltic ports and back, meant covering a distance of 4,000 nautical miles, leaving only 3,000 for the combat zone, an insufficient distance if we consider that its mission of hunting meant covering large distances. Even though the possibility of leaving from ports along the Atlantic coast gave an increased margin, the United States entry into the war posed the problem of the 5,000 nautical miles needed to reach the South Atlantic.

After 1942, the autonomy was increased to 18,000 nautical miles (at 6 knots), which allowed only a maximum of three weeks operations in the Caribbean Sea, even without re-supply, making it essential to be re-supplied from the sea if the missions were to be profitable. It was for this reason that the 2,000 metric ton submarines were designed, the famous « Milk Cows », designed for supplying

above
U-124, commanded by KL Wilhelm Schulz, being refuelled with diesel by the raider *Kormoran*.
(ECPAD/DAM 1082 L37)

left
« *What all crew members of a German submarine must know.* » This is a popularised booklet teaching the basics.
(F. Bachmann collection)

food, fuel and torpedoes for ten combat submarines. For all that, one should not overestimate the problems caused by the lesser autonomy of these vessels. Indeed, although the large submarines could remain at sea for longer periods, the physical endurance of the crew was difficult to prolong and remained limited by time. After two months, they had to return.

Stored in the holds, the diesel, once used, had to be replaced in order to keep the boat's balance. The holds were made in such a way that sea water could go over the bottom valve that was placed at the lowest point of the

above
A close up of the outside of the hull. One can see the circular water inlets and outlets on the lower section.
(DR)

boat and opened during the sorties. Diesel is lighter than sea water, and it floated on the top, from where it was pumped towards the engines. A simple system that needed, however, the level of the holds to be closely watched in order to avoid pumping sea water that when mixed with fuel in combustion, left a slight white mist in the exhaust fumes.

If the limits brought about by the fuel could be lived with, the same could not be said for a lack of torpedoes, especially at the beginning of the war when the Allies had not yet began to fight back. The U-Boote could quickly use all their torpedoes, U-99, during one of its missions only spent nine days at sea, four to reach its objective, 24 hours of fighting where it used all of its torpedoes in the destruction of nine ships, and four days to return to base. Some submarines, once they had used all of their torpedoes were ordered to remain in the area in order to carry out weather reports for the Luftwaffe. However, this sort of side mission could only be a stop-gap.

Efforts were therefore made to increase the number of these precious weapons that could be carried. Although the Type VII C at the beginning only carried 14 torpedoes (it ended up by carrying 21 in 1941), the Type IX would carry 22 (Type A and B), with 24 for the Type D.

As well as those stored in the boat, some were stored in pressurised cases on the deck ; this only partially resolved the problem as it was necessary to surface to load these torpedoes, which in a combat zone was rarely without danger. Loading the torpedoes with a hoist on the oblique plane of the loading hatch took 30 long minutes. The obvious solution was to save as many torpedoes as possible and to finish off unarmed ships with the deck gun. This, however, became rapidly impossible with development of escorts. The submarine was manoeuvrable and also a relatively fast surface vessel that could sail at 17 knots (32 kph), its maximum under water speed was only 8 knots (15 kph).

The power plant, placed at the rear, took up a lot of the boat's space ; they were of two types, diesel and electric. The diesel room had

above
Sleeve insignia for a Mechnikersmaat (able seaman) Torpedomechanikerlaufbahn (torpedo mechanic branch).
(F. Bachmann collection)

right
Close up of the diesel engine for a Type VII submarine.
(P. de Romanovsky collection)

two engines, (port and starboard) which were given names by the Commander or the LI (Leitender Ingenieur, or chief mechanic), the first of these to go aboard a new submarine. These names sometimes evoked the regions from where they came from (Thünnes und Schäl for the Rheinlanders, Hummel und Mors for the Hamburgers), there were, however, names like Max und Moritz, Rabatz und Klamauk, Tran und Helle, Dick und Dolle, and phonetically, on U-172, Rackel und Dackel.

In the zone of operations, these engines were operated alternately, every four hours, so that

above
The crew loads a torpedo into the submarine via the hatch. This manoeuvre was particularly delicate due to the size of the torpedoes and the small size of the hatch through which they were loaded. This limited size which made the loading of torpedoes tricky, was, however, an indispensable guarantee of strength for the submarine.
(ECPAD)

they would share an equal workload and in order to save the precious fuel. This technique also ensured that they were always warm and ready to go at full speed. These high speeds were achieved by using both motors when full speed was required. The different speeds (half ahead, full ahead, full speed ahead) propelled the vessel from 14 to 18 knots, the engines then turned at 600 revs per minute and could be backed up by the electric motors in an emergency. These eight cylinder engines, taller than a man, were made by MAN and were very reliable when at sea, break downs were a rare occurrence. When running, they recharged the batteries of the electric motors that allowed under water navigation.

When submerged, the electric motors took over as they did not use the submarine's oxygen reserves. The fifty metric tons of stored batteries were placed in the two battery compartments (Akkuraum 1, at the stern, just under the petty officers' quarters and Akkuraum 2 at the bow, under the officers' quarters) and required three hours on the surface to be recharged. Their maintenance was particularly difficult with only 60 cm of space between the top of the batteries and the floors of the quarters. The sailor whose job it was to check the level of the batteries had to move around laying flat on a trolley. This form of power was essential for moving under water but also for keeping the submarine at the desired depth.

Contrary to common opinion, a stationary U-Boot would not float but sink. Using the dive planes and the lateral planes, the current created by the speed and the pressure placed on them, allowed the vessel to surface or dive. For a U-Boot to remain under water and keep its trim, it was essential to maintain a weak speed which was enough for the forward and above all, aft dive planes to be efficient ❑

The victorious crew of U-333
parade through the streets
of La Rochelle.
(P-M Rousseau collection)

THE MEN AND THE MACHINES

THE COMMANDERS AND THEIR CREWS

The U-Boote commanders were, for the most part, young men, of a rank that was more often equivalent to lieutenant. Although the « Kaleunt » (Kapitänleutnant) are symbolic of the submarine armcommanders, the officers who carried out the duties of watch officer could be much younger. Dönitz's own son, Peter, was only 21 when he cast off for his first wartime mission aboard U-954 as watch officer. At the end of the war, faced with the carnage made possible by the progress of allied under water detection systems and the offensive tactics of Admiral Max Horton, certain young officers were immediately placed in the role of commander. In this way, reserve Oberleutnant zur See Hans-Georg Hess, became the youngest commander in the history of the German Navy, by taking command of U-466 only a few months after his 21st birthday. Despite the legend, for a long time given credence by historians and the U-Boote commanders themselves, these were not men just out of their teenage years. The lowest average is 26 years and seven months (1942 and 1944), at the beginning of the war in 1939 to 1940 it was 29 years and five months. As the British submarine « ace », Rear Admiral Ben Bryant said, the best age to command a submarine was between 25 and 30, « *old enough to be experienced, to be confident in oneself and one's judgement, young enough not to think too much.* »

above
At Lorient, Admiral Dönitz, BdU, invites the commanders to the château de Kernevel to hear their mission reports. Even though they are several ranks below him, he listens to their reports with neither preconceived opinion nor prejudice, conscious of the progress that only experience can bring. Later on, when the BdU moved, he was not able to carry out this essential task, the same applied to his successor, Admiral von Friedeburg.
(ECPAD/DAM 1085 L4)

right
Officers and crew members of U-53 gathered around their commander, Kapitänleutnant Russe, during the Great War. Certain veterans were obviously made to contribute to the training of those called to succeed them.
(DR/P-M Rousseau collection)

following page top
The much sought after Knights Cross of the Iron Cross.
(Militaria Magazine)

following page bottom
A booklet for the identification of the world's ships.
(P-M Rousseau collection)

Training for submarines was obviously carried out by First World War veterans, such as Kapitän sur See Bruno Mahn, who was a coastal submarine commander at the end of the Great War, or Korvettenkapitän Friedrich Schäfer, watch officer on U-55 in the North Atlantic in 1918. However, some officers went back on combat missions at a venerable age. Georg von Wilamowitz-Möllendorf, a 24 year old watch officer in August 1917, went back to sea as

commander of U-459 at the age of 48. He commanded this « Milk Cow » for two years, before disappearing on July 24th, 1943 after being attacked by two British Wellington bombers.

Those who presented themselves as men of « Dönitz's Volunteer Corps », literally worshipped their leader, familiarly known as « The Lion ». It is true that the latter (named Befehlshaber der U-Boote — BdU — or Commander of the Submarine Fleet since September 19th, 1939), cultivated his aura by meeting commanders in person when they returned from a patrol so that they could share their opinions with him and possible improvements (at least during his time at Lorient). This method was above all based on Dönitz's unshakable conviction that sea and combat experience was irreplaceable and that it alone allowed the accumulation of decisive information for a more efficient use of the submarine arm. It maintained an essential personal link between the leader and his subordinates who

was automatically awarded after 100,000 tons. The longer serving sailors did not hesitate in running away from these young commanders by volunteering for service with more experienced commanders, the « Lebensversicherungen » (life insurance), who did not hesitate in taking great risks to save men from the sea. This did not apply to all and some did not hesitate in abandoning the men on watch to their fate when faced with a crash dive. Despite the legend that surrounds the personality of Gunther Prien, it would appear that the Commander of U-47 belongs to the this category. Magnified by his exploit at Scapa Flow, he was in fact little appreciated by his officers and utterly disliked by his crew who had to carry out useless exercises once back in port, whilst he would happily disappear until re-embarkation. However, more than their altruism, it was their competence that was the foundation of their authority, and this was not only in favour of the members of the crew. The Americans who captured U-128 in May 1943, were alarmed to see that the First Watch Officer, Siegfried Sterzing, had effectively taken over command of the boat from his commander Hermann Steinart, the latter having accepted his subordination due to Sterzing's experience. In the same way, Midshipman Horst Bredow, when boarding U-288 that was finishing off its training in the Baltic in September 1943, was given a choice by his commander, Oberleutnant zur See Willy Meyer. He could either play at being an officer or learn the realities of life aboard a submarine. After having bravely chosen the latter, that made him share anonymously, for six weeks, the life of the crew, he was rewarded by his commander who took him on as his Second Watch Officer.

Not everyone had the humility of the young Horst Bredow and many young commanders dreamed of renewing the exploits of their glorious elders, the famous « aces » of 1940-1941, like Prien, Kretschmer, Schepke (reputed to have fiddled with the sunk tonnage registers so that he could keep up with the other two), Lüth, or Endras, whose performances owed much to their tacti-

directly confronted their enemy. The frankness of the submariners with their leader, even though they were five or six ranks lower than him, shocked members of other General Staffs. A Luftwaffe general, visiting the Admiral's H.Q. at Kernevel, Lorient, left completely flabbergasted by the sharpness of the talk and the content of the points of view that were exchanged around the table. This was, however, the price to be paid for the way in which the future Grossadmiral commanded his men, some of whom took great pleasure in openly flouting military convention.

Most of them stood out by their audacity and ambition. The latter often made the crew wary of them, worrying about the zeal and ill considered audacity with which these new recruits went about winning decorations. The sailors called these ambitious men « Draufgänger » (a go-getter) or « Halsschmerzen », literally meaning a sore throat, hinting at the much sought after Knight's Cross of the Iron Cross. The tonnage race was begun with even more impatience as this decoration

above
U-47 and its commander, Gunther Prien, the « Bull of Scapa Flow ».
(DR)

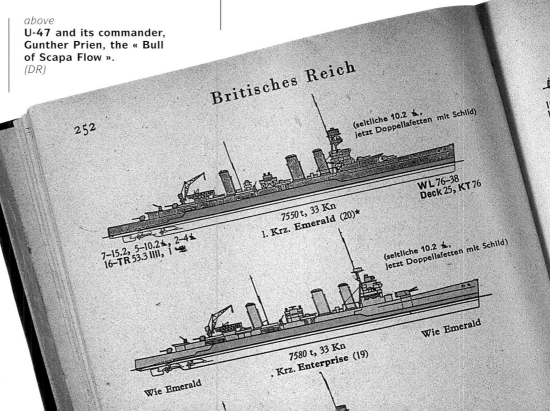

left
Oberleutnant zur See Engelbert Endrass. *(DR)*

right
Kapitänleutnant Joachim Schepke. He was an officer at Stralsund from October 1936 to March 1937, then an instructor at the Flensburg-Mürwick torpedo school from March 1937 to October 1938. *(DR)*

below
Cap insignia of U-92. It undertook five enemy patrols and was put out of service on October 12th, 1944 after being bombed by British planes.
(F. Bachmann collection)

below
U-46 of Oberleutnant zur See Engelbert Endrass, which adopted the « Bull of Scapa Flow » emblem, a reminder of the time he served as first watch officer on Prien's U-47, entering the port with a damaged bridge caused by an accident.
(DR)

cal skill but also to the slowness of an Allied ability to hit back. Not all came from the Navy, Prien learnt his trade in the Merchant Navy (after having joined a sailing ship as ship's boy at the age of 16, then as a deck sailor on a merchant ship, he passed his Merchant Navy officer's exam before becoming captain at the age of 24. It was only in 1933 that he left the Merchant Navy for the Navy, and after passing through the submarine school at Kiel, boarded U-26 as Watch Officer. Apart from the personnel who came from the Merchant Navy, some came from the General Staffs of the Surface Fleet (Fregattenkapitän Jürgen Wattenberg), or aviation (Kapitänleutnant Manfred Kinzel or Otto Werner).

This audacity was not without its dilemmas and it is still difficult today to determine how they all got on. Indeed how do you conciliate the laws that were unwritten but held dear by all sailors, the helping of shipwrecked men and the cruel necessities of submarine warfare, reaffirmed by the orders of Dönitz? After the

JOACHIM SCHEPKE (1912-1941)

He began his navy officer career in April 1930 and, after his first posting on the cruiser *Deutschland*, he joined the submarine arm in October 1935. After spending 18 months as an instructor at the Flensburg torpedo school, he took command of one of the new navy's first U-Boot, U-3. He was then given the command of U-19 with which he sank 9 Allied ships, then the Type VII B U-100. It was with this boat that he covered himself in glory during his second patrol when he sank seven ships for a total of more than 50,000 metric tons, an exploit which earned him the Knight's Cross of the Iron Cross. On November 23rd, he managed the same exploit and once more, sank seven Allied ships with a displacement of more than 24,000 metric tons. It was after this new exploit that he was awarded oak leaves. A figurehead of the regime, he published, in 1940, a book entitled « U-Boot Fahrer von heute » (U-boat men of today), in which he wrote about life on board, illustrated with his own pictures. Nicknamed, for his good looks, *Ihrer Majestät bestaussehender Offizier* (His Majesty's best-looking officer), he did not hesitate in defending the regime and the submarine war at the Berlin sports hall in February 1941. He was killed when his boat was rammed by *HMS Vanoc* on March 17th, 1941. Of the 44 crew members of U-100, only six were saved from the water.

drama of the *Laconia* in September 1942, where the attacking submarine, U-156, was machine gunned by an American plane after having rescued survivors, the « Triton Null » order became imperative. It was now forbidden for commanders to « *try to save people on a torpedoed ship, to rescue men from the water and take them to a boat, to right overturned lifeboats, to give food and water. Rescue is in contradiction to most elementary principal of war which is the destruction of enemy ships and crews.* »

above
The survivors of the *Atlantis*, rescued by U-126, were an additional threat and dilemma. Once they were on the deck, the submarine could not dive without taking with him the prisoners whose deaths would have made the commander a war criminal.
(ECPAD/DAM 985 L30)

below left
After torpedoing the *Atlantis*, U-68 recovered the prisoners, some of whom were towed behind in their lifeboats.
(ECPAD/DAM 978 L4)

right
Cap insignia of U-979.
(P. de Romanovsky collection)

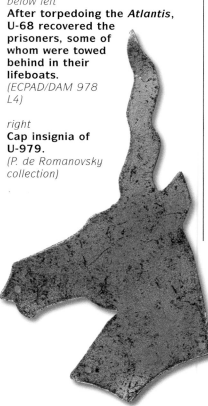

In reality it would appear that Dönitz ordered his men to abandon survivors to their fate at the end of 1939. His permanent order N° 154 was indeed unambiguous, « *Do not take anyone aboard. Do not worry about lifeboats. Weather conditions or proximity to the coast do not in anyway count. Look after your submarine and try to obtain a new success as soon as possible. We have to be hard in this war.* »

Although some ignored these orders (notably in the case of commanders Siegmann of U-230 and Altmeier of U-1227, who refused to sink escorts that had stopped to pick up survivors), others were less scrupulous like commander Eck of U-852, who fired on survivors so that they would not signal his presence, an act for which he was fired with his officers in Germany after the war.

ACCOUNT OF A SURVIVOR

This is an account by one of the survivors of the merchant ship *Roxborough Castle* which was sunk on February 22nd, 1943 north west of the Azores by U-107 commanded by Kapitänleutnant Harald Gelhaus.
« *The commander of the U-Boot asked us (in perfect English) if we were wounded, if we needed food or water, or if we needed anything at all. We thanked him after replying in the negative to his questions. He then apologized for having sunk us and told us how far we were from the closest island, giving us the heading to take. He wished us good luck and disappeared.* »

Seeing that the chances of putting out the fire that had broken out on board, no doubt after the explosion of a torpedo, were nil, the men leave the ship as quickly as possible in order to escape from the blast of the explosion. *(P. de Romanovsky collection)*

This is the only known example, even if it is certain that some events were not written down in the ship's log, it nevertheless remains that the moral dilemmas that were posed by this situation had serious consequences for these young men who knew that once the survivors had been picked up, the escorts would once again hunt them down.

Death was, therefore, omnipresent in the life of a submariner, be it their own imminent demise or that which they had just inflicted. However, and this was already observed during the First World War, the men mana-

below
The death announcement of Kapitänleutnant Helmuth Ringelmann, commander of U-75 which disappeared in the Mediterranean near Marsa-Matruh (Egypt) on December 28th, 1941. He was posthumously promoted to Korvettenkapitän. *(P. de Romanovsky collection)*

right
A French made (Bacqueville) submarine war badge. The metal is of a poor quality and the cardboard case denotes a late manufacture. *(F. Bachmann collection)*

ged to keep their emotions at a distance which corresponded to the ever larger distances between fighting men. They were targets, planes and ships, much more than men, that had to be destroyed. It was tonnage that was added up, more than the corresponding human lives. All mention of the fate of survivors of torpedoed ships was avoided on board the subma-

rine. The crews of American submarines in the Pacific, who incidentally acted in exactly the same way as the Germans, adopted the same voluntary blindness. The death of a submariner did not have quite the same meaning as a soldier on the Eastern Front. Indeed, in the opposite of the latter who lived in a world of blood, amputations and various mutilations, death was perceived as a distant entity. When a submarine was lost at sea, no bodies were found, no debris, as if death did not exist.

Even if all were not politically committed, one needs to be careful with the self proclaimed post war non political stand that was carefully maintained by Dönitz and submariners of every country. Some like Prien or Schepke, did not hesitate in accepting the support of the regime that rewarded their devotion by making them national heroes, idolised by the people. Apart from the symbolic rewards, nothing was too good for these icons of National Socialism. On the other hand, harsh treatment was meted out to those who showed their opposition to the regime and its leaders too openly. Such was the case with Oberleutnant Kusch of U- 154, who upon returning from a patrol in December 1943, was denounced by his First Watch Officer, Oberleutnant zur See Abel, who pointed out his lack of fighting spirit and his demoralizing attitude as well as his acid remarks made against the Nazi party and the Führer (the portrait of whom he had removed from the boat). Sentenced to be stripped of his rank and shot, he was executed the following May 12th after his sentence was confirmed by Dönitz.

However, all the talk of the intensity of the political commitment or, on the contrary, its absence, should be taken with great caution. Naturally protected by their particular position, far from the choices that their army comrades were faced with, notably in the pitiless repression of civilian populations, the sailors fought and died for an ideology that had a minor impact on their day to day existence and way of fighting. Although some officers were, at the beginning, fanatically convinced by the National Socialist ideology, a great many changed their way of thinking during the war compared to their original opinions. This was nota-

above
A victory pennant. The tonnage of 9,325 corresponds to a large merchant ship.
(P-M Rousseau collection)

right
Submarine commanders were particularly pampered by the regime, at least until the first half of 1943.
(ECPAD)

below
The cemetery at Lorient in the middle of the war illustrates the losses suffered by the German submariners, the port included ! (at sea, by definition there is no grave... « Roses don't grow on a sailor's grave... »).
(ECPAD/DAM 953 L9)

bly the case with Eric Topp who joined the NSDAP in May 1933 before integrating the SS in 1934 but who became more and more critical of the regime at the end of the war. Opposite to this is Joachim Schepke who only joined the Nazi Party after having integrated the Navy, in his memoirs he shows an anti-Semitism and an absolute faith in the principles of National Socialism. The differences between

Raeder and Dönitz also show the evolution of the German Navy with regards to the regime. If in both cases, obedience was an un-passable horizon, Raeder's opportunism, sometimes made of his resistance to Hitler's designs, contrasted singularly with Dönitz's unconditional adherence to the regime. The latter, although he fully approved of the Führerprinzip, showed an unconditional loyalty mixed with fascination for Hitler, not hesitating to write in August 1943, that « *whoever thinks he can do better than the Führer is a madman.* »

There are plenty of examples of commanders who stood out by their refusal to embrace the regime's ideology, despite the risks this entailed. In July 1943, Kapitänleutnant Werner Henke, owed his freedom to the personal apology that Dönitz made to Hitler. It took all of the Grossadmiral's diplomacy to convince Hitler not to arrest one of his « aces » who had just called the men of the Innsbruck Gestapo gangsters

for having mistreated some of his friends. In a cheekier way, Fregattenkapitän Reinhard Suhren became well known for his insolence, arriving carefully at the dock in Brest with U-564, he shouted through a loudhailer to the crowd waiting on the quay, asking them if the Nazis were still « *in power* ». When everyone replied that they were, he put the engines into reverse and moved away from the quay to general mirth.

Generally, one should be wary of the uniform view of these officers that all seem to come from the same mould. Although their courage is not to be doubted, any hesitations or mistakes of command could be severely punished. Some were simply stripped of their responsibilities by Dönitz, who deemed that they were not carrying out their duties correctly (Kapitänleutnant Heinicke or Frantzke), others paid dearly for their mistakes. Kapitänleutnant Hirsacker who had already failed to get through Gibraltar in 1941 and who, during the Allied landings in North Africa in November 1942, was accused of cowardice in the face of the enemy, was court-martialled, condemned to death in April 1943. (He commited suicide before his execution)

On the other hand, and in the pure navy tradition, some refused to accept defeat and preferred to go down with their ship. Kapitänleutnant Kapitsky, after having ensured his crew's safety, went back into his boat (U-615) and sank with it in August 1943, following the example of the 50 year old First World War veteran, Korvettenkapitän Georg von Wilamowitz-Möllendorf, who went down with U-459 in the July of the same year. Faced with desperate situations, some did not hesitate in putting dying men out of their misery before

GROSSADMIRAL ERICH RAEDER (1876-1960)

Admiral Hipper's Chief of Staff in 1914-1918, he took part in the famous battles of Dogger Bank and Jutland before taking command of the cruiser *Köln* in 1918. He continued his brilliant career in the years between the wars, his skills recognised both by the Weimar Republic and the national socialist regime. He became head of the Kriegsmarine in 1938 and sought to make it, within the framework of the Z plan, a powerful surface fleet. Faced with the disappointing results of the large warships, which contrasted with the feats of the U-Boote, Admiral Dönitz succeeded him on January 30th, 1943. Despite his background role as Inspector General of the Navy, he was put on trial at Nuremberg and sentenced to life imprisonment. He was released in 1955.

top
Kapitänleutnant Erich Topp. Rising to the command of a flotilla in September 1942, he later became the leader of a U-Boote trials section and he finished the war as commander of U-2513, a revolutionary Type XXI submarine.
(DR)

above
Grossadmiral Erich Raeder.
(ECPAD/DAM 56 L20)

top right
This car pennant was flown from the left wing of the vehicle, from the rank of lieutenant commander. An example can be seen in the photograph above.
(Private collection)

REINHARD SUHREN (1916-1984)

Beginning his career in the submarine arm in March 1938, he served as first watch officer on U-48 under commander Schultze, winning the Knight's Cross. However, he had to wait until April 1941 to be named as commander of U-564 with which he sank the British corvette, *HMS Zinnia* in August 1941. In September 1942, the oak leaves and swords were added to his Knight's Cross. He was named as instructor in the October of the same year. During the course of the last year of the war, he was successively named as commander in chief of U-Boote for the Norwegian theatre then for the North Sea.

committing suicide themselves. After an attack, the Commander of U-604, Horst Höltring, shot himself in the head after having shot two of his men, mortally wounded by the chlorine fumes of the batteries. Cases of suicide, however, were rare, apart from Höltring, we know of the case of Kapitänleutnant Peter Zshech of U-505 in October 1942, and the failed attempt of Kapitänleutnant Wenzel of U-231 in January 1944. There must have been other cases but they were not witnessed. It is very tempting to praise this representation of the Commander going down with his ship as with the example of Commander Langsdorff. It is, however, certain that the exploitation of ending one's life in this way, in the tradition of a fantastical code of honour, corresponded fully to the pure and heroic image that the critics of the submarine arm, post war, wanted to portray for posterity.

above
Kapitänleutnant Reinhard Suhren.
(DR)

below
U-505, with its conning tower completely destroyed, could not dive and was abandoned by its crew which did not manage to scuttle it. A boarding party took it. It was taken to the United States where it was displayed at Chicago as a war trophy at the end of the war.
(Private collection)

Globally, the examples of physical courage greatly outweigh those of blatant cowardice given that an integral part of these officers' training was in dealing with extreme situations. The principal off surface attacks at night meant that they had to get as close to the target as possible with the risk of being spotted, when diving, by the escorts. This would mean being hunted, and whatever their skill in evading the enemy, they could not be guaranteed of escaping. Learning to control fear, one's own and that of the crew became an essential part of a good commander. This was all the more true if the submarine was damaged, faced with the panic which could follow, the Commander had to show calm in order to avoid it spreading throughout the boat, definitively paralysing the men. Situations sometimes demanded exceptional resistance, as shown by the Commander of U-167, Alfred Brandi who, after a loss of power caused by a depth charge, was trampled by his men who were running away from the chlorine fumes of the batteries. Managing to get up, he reached the command post and re-took control of his crew. In some rare cases, men lost their cool and completely broke down nervously. The commander of U-505, Kapitänleutnant Peter Zschech, after a year as Watch Officer and another as commander, committed suicide whilst being pursued by escorts in October 1943.

It is true that the crews were fiercely attached to their commanders, despite the reservations they had about their audacity. This attachment was often reciprocated, the Commander, who often used his right, when he

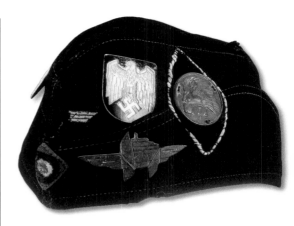

was given command of a new boat to take with him men who he deemed necessary to the smooth running of the boat, gladly saw himself as the father of his men. This freedom given to the Commander meant avoiding a high turnover of crew members, keeping certain veterans was a mark of stability and meant that newcomers could benefit from their experience. This freedom, however, was sometimes thwarted by the necessities of service and the development of the submarine arm that meant

above and below
The commander surrounded by his men on land, a composition which was particularly appreciated by the regime which willingly took on men who, following the example of Suhren seen here, were never totally taken in by it. Below, Commander Lehmann-Willenbrock with his men, back from a campaign.
(DR)

that the most tenacious commanders had to let a certain number of their veterans go, their experience being needed within new crews. U-515, during the twenty months of its existence (August 1942-April 1944), took on a hundred men, of whom 34 served for ten months, with only 19 who remained on board during the entire period.

Managing a crew obviously varied greatly with the individual personalities of the Commanders, but it was most of the time characterised by a great flexibility. It was not surprising, therefore, that Fregattenkapitän Lüth, well known for his benevolence, was made head of the submarine school, cleverly teaching just

top right
A model 1939 dark blue cloth Bordmütze. It was worn by petty officers, leading rates and sailors. This example belonged to a member of U-66.
(P-M Rousseau collection)

following page
A mess or home plaque. « *In memory of my patrols against the enemy on U-218* **». This boat was part of the 9th U-Flotille. It fell into Allied hands at Bergen, Norway on May 8th, 1945.** *(P-M Rousseau collection)*

exactly what should be the relationship between the Commander and his crew, even going so far as to write letters to the girlfriends or parents of the men who could not read or write. Far from being a model of Prussian rigidity, he used anything that did not put the submarine's crew in danger, which was seen as a real community. He also refused to write a man's name down in the punishment log book if it risked compromising his chance of further promotion, instead he preferred to pin up the list of punishments in the latrines so that everyone would see them rather than making it more dramatic by being secret. His philosophy of command can be summed up in one sentence, « *it is the duty of every captain to have faith in his men, even if they have disappointed him at one time or another.* »

On the other hand he could be pitiless with regards to what he saw as breaking the contract that linked the members of the community. The finding of alcohol (which in theory was forbidden aboard), squirreling away a personal store of food from that of the boat, insubordination or violence, all were immediately punished. Although some were sent to sleep on the iron sheeting or made to peel potatoes, the confiscation of a deck of cards or cutting off the offender from the rest of the crew (the crew were not allowed to talk to him), could be just as efficient. In a closed world, where the lack of privacy could be suffocating, being cut off from the others was often all it needed to calm things down.

The mystical strength of the German submarine arm was due to having been successful in creating a particularly original link between commanders and their crews. Far from being a straightforward relation of orders and obedience at work, these were personal relationships which united the Commanders and their men. This cult of comradeship was even more necessary in that the communion that stemmed from the interior of the group made for an greater combat efficiency. As Dönitz said, it was only when this community was established that one could see the appearance, « *in the midst of this military community, the spiritual attitude of the true soldier. The belief, both conscious and subconscious, that there are higher goals than one's own life and therefore the readiness of the individual to be truly committed and risk his life to save or protect others* ». This explains why the submariners fought to the end, justifying the British government's official report on the Battle of the Atlantic which stated that, « *until the bitter end, the German submarines fought with discipline and*

above
A group photo of an officer surrounded by his crew. Unlike the traditional photos on the deck with all the crew, the photographer has shown some of the men at their work stations.
(DR)

efficiency. There was no letting up in their efforts nor any hesitation on their part in exposing themselves to danger. »

For Dönitz, and more globally, for all the naval officers of his generation that had lived through the traumatism of 1918 mutinies, this ideal community was essential. Apart from the fact of it being an essential asset in combat, it also kept away the spectre of mutinies happening

tary protocol. Nevertheless, discreet signs enabled each man's function to be identified without this really being seen as an element of uniform. In this way, all officers and Chief Petty Officers wore a blue peaked cap whilst junior Petty Officers were identified by gold braid on their collars.

This community was even more closely bonded in that all the men were essential on a submarine and no one who was not necessary was on board. Even if it was not rare for a submarine to take passengers, the fact that they led to overcrowding or that they sometimes took the place of a useful sailor meant that they were seen as intruders, only tolerated when they were not outside elements. For these sailors, used to living under the gaze of the next man, they only accepted those who shared their destiny. Weather specialists, navy doctors, technicians, members of the B-Dienst, public relations officers, war correspondents or photographers that went on board were often teased, when they were not openly ostracized.

The U-Boote could even take on board political personalities. U-180 commanded by Kapitän zur See Werner Musenberg, took on board the Indian nationalist leader Chandra Bose in order to meet up with a Japanese submarine in the Indian Ocean. There were even cases of taking on board intelligence officers, saboteurs

again. As he had observed that the ships which remained untouched by the events of 1918 were all of small size and submarines, Dönitz justified his original approach to command, based on the flexibility of the hierarchical relationships, which was symbolically expressed via the unorthodox wearing of badges of rank, which of course did not signify that they did not exist. They simply had to appear as something which was obviously accepted and not as a constraint to be endured... Unlike the surface crews, there was not the discipline and caste system which was typical of the Prussian mentality. Also, the lack of physical privacy on board meant that adjustments had to be made to mili-

July 1941, the men of U-69 upon their return to Saint-Nazaire, wear magnificent panama hats, no doubt found in some crates floating amongst the wreckage of a ship sent to the bottom.
(ECPAD/DAM 88 L13)

above
Certain personalities were invited on board submarines to see the « aces » of the German Navy. Accompanied by an army officer, the Norwegian writer, Knut Hamsun, goes along with the propaganda machine.
(ECPAD/DAT 4315 32)

or teams of commandos ; the latter was, however, a relatively rare occurrence. Of the 2,700 surviving logbooks, only 25 mention this type of embarkation, on the other hand they more often took on board crews of torpedo boats (60 logbooks), sunk or damaged Axis vessels (32), shot down Axis planes (14). The most unusual was certainly the case of Kapitänleutnant Josef Röther's U-380 which rescued four German infantrymen from the Tunisian coast on May 10th, 1943 at the end of the Tunisian campaign. In these last cases, space was found in the crew positions and officers and crew gladly gave up their bunks.

This community, when faced with adversity, acted as one block. It was not surprising, therefore, that when survivors of a destroyed submarine were interrogated by the Allies, hardly any would talk. Gallery, the future American admiral, chief of the Task Force Guadalcanal, thus wrote at having « *never been able to get from submarine prisoners anything more than their name, rank and number of their submarine* ».

It was an entire corps that defended itself from exterior aggression, right up to defeat and capture. It is true that they were, at least for some crews, largely fanatical. After the interrogation of the first of the German « aces » to be captured, Hans Jenisch of U-32 in October 1940, the conclusions drawn by the British officers on the men that they had just interrogated were without any doubt. They thus summed up that they « *were all fanatical Nazis. The had a deep hatred of the English, which was not so obvious with previously captured crews. They are all for total war and believe in the justification of violence, cruelty, breaking treaties or other crimes as long as it serves*

the advent of the German race in Europe. In their minds, the success of 1940 has not made Hitler the equal of God, they have made him God himself ! »

When in February 1941, the survivors of U-70, which had been rammed by a Dutch tanker, were interrogated by an English officer, he stated that, « *the morale of the officers and*

above
Even though U-Boote were not troop transport vessels, some had to carry out intelligence or commando missions. This was notably the case of KL Linder's U-202 which, on June 13th, 1942, as part of operation « Pastorius », landed four agents at Amagansett-Long Island. *(DR)*

men is high, they show no sign of weariness when talking of the war and repeat ad nauseam the slogans of their disgusting propaganda. » This observation seems to contradict Hitler's saying that « *The Army was reactionary, the Air Force National Socialist and the Navy Christian.* » The capture of Kretschmer's crew in March 1941 seems to corroborate this view concerning that of the officer's corps. Although the midshipmen, who were there at

the beginning of the war in 1939, showed themselves as being strongly pro Nazi, opening their mouths only to spout the text of the official propaganda, the older officers, including Kretschmer and his Second Officer, Hans Jochen von Knebel Döberitz (had previously been Flag Lieutenant to Dönitz), finally showed

themselves to be fairly disillusioned and seemed to show more loyalty to their social class and their country than to their government.

It would, however, be absurd, to form an opinion based solely on these observations, which reflects, moreover, the image that Nazi propaganda wished to substantiate. Thus,

above
Two Royal Navy patrol boats return from a night patrol on the North Sea. After having crippled a U-Boot, the latter had to surface and its crew surrender. The two officers seen here are taken away blindfolded to be interrogated.
(IWM)

right
Cap insignia of U-591.
(P. de Romanovsky collection)

left
The men of a sunken submarine are going to be recovered by an American ship which will drop a net which the survivors can use to climb on board. However, the rescuer's outstretched hands will mercilessly push them away if they refuse to give their boat's number, rank or if they refuse to say whether they are an isolated boat or part of a wolf pack which will strike again. Despite the vital necessity for escort vessels to know precisely the nature of the threat facing the convoy they were protecting, very few accepted this infringement of the brotherhood of seamen without qualms.
(National Archives)

whereas it is true that the crew was mostly made up of volunteers, Petty Officers were often so rare that they were forcibly enrolled. In January 1942, the results of interrogations of captured submariners revealed that « *most of the prisoners mentioned with revulsion their service on board a submarine, which differed greatly from what the propaganda had promised. These seems to imply that the crews are not always made up of volunteers.* » In reality, if the majority of those who had joined the Navy had chosen this arm, it was not with hope of joining the submarines, but rather that of avoiding the Eastern Front, as part of a service that was traditionally presumed to be at less risk. According to an account by a petty officer, crews were made up of authentic volunteers until 1942, then a little less after.

Those skilled in a technical speciality were the first to be sent to the submarine arm, from the spring of 1940, without them being asked what they preferred. Radio Operator Wolfgang Hirschfeld, who enlisted in 1936 as a Radio Operator on a torpedo boat, was made to go on submarines in April 1940, his only choice being that of which type of boat he wished to serve on. Senior Petty Officers in charge of propulsion (Obermaschinisten), if they passed the medical tests, were directly allotted to the U-Boote.

Those who had completed the four year period, which they had initially signed up for, and who did not wish to prolong, were sometimes automatically chosen by their section head to prolong their service. A report described their situation. « *Most accepted. They were better off than those who did not follow their example and who found themselves with papers stamped with " has abandoned the Fatherland in danger" when they left the Navy at the end of their period of service. With this stamped on the papers it was impossible to find work. A prisoner continually repeated that once the Navy had you, that was it.* » It was not uncommon that some were there against their will, caught up in the logic of propaganda and the need to conform. A young conscript who had just been caught by the English declared that, « *at Kiel, they did all that they could to make submarines popular. But I had promised at home that I would not join the submarine arm and when they asked us "who wants to join the submarines?" I thought, no, I won't do it. But they put their hands up one after the other and my friend said to me "put your hand up, let's join up together"; I still thought no. So he took my hand and he lifted it up when it was our turn and they took both our names. So I said to myself, maybe I'll have more luck in the tests, but I was taken on.* »

However, one has to be careful with the accounts gathered by the British after having captured a U-Boot. It is very probable that some men, exhausted after a long chase, felt the temptation to distance themselves from a vanquished and vulnerable crew. And if it is certain that German propaganda over-exaggerated the enthusiasm of the young recruit for the submarine, it would be unrealistic to assume that the proportion of unwilling men within a crew was nothing other than a very small minority. To have a large number of these men on board would have been in all cases a danger to the safety of the crew. It should be noted that there was never a recruitment crisis for submarines ; in 1944, only 37 % of applicants fulfilled the recruitment criteria and were selected.

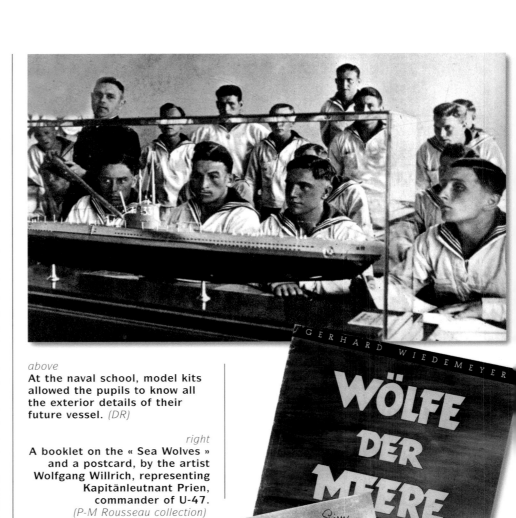

above
At the naval school, model kits allowed the pupils to know all the exterior details of their future vessel. *(DR)*

right
A booklet on the « Sea Wolves » and a postcard, by the artist Wolfgang Willrich, representing Kapitänleutnant Prien, commander of U-47.
(P-M Rousseau collection)

below
Although the commander was the only one to be awarded the Knights Cross, it was not uncommon for the whole crew to be decorated for its participation in a boat's feat of arms. In March 1941, Commander Lehmann-Willenbrock decorated all his men with the Iron Cross.
(ECPAD/DAM 865 L10)

In reality, the sense of belonging to an elite, convinced of its superiority, worked for many, in a very attractive way. The English report concerning Kretschmer's crew, was, in this respect very revealing. It concluded that the men, « *had an exaggerated feeling of their superiority and dignity. These excessive opinions no doubt came from the public adulation which they were used to, they had special planes and bouquets of flowers at each station when they were on leave.* » It is also true that returning from missions in the summer of 1940 and the spring of 1941 corresponded to a happy period « die glückliche Zeit ». The crews were awaited for by a crowd that welcomed them with flowers and a brass band, presents and applause if the Commander received a decoration. Submariners ended the war with the record of awards of the Knight's Cross of the Iron Cross, this record is even more

U-96 returning to Brest, its home port. A large crowd gets ready to celebrate and pamper its heroes. The latter will once more be able to enjoy a few glasses of alcohol, wash and sleep in clean sheets.
(P-M Rousseau collection)

at the *Pigeon Blanc* hotel. The officers' mess, at the Préfecture which had been turned into a headquarters, was also where the meals took place for returning crews, such as that held for Kretschmer and his men, invited to dine around a horseshoe shaped table, the emblem of their submarine.

A special train, naturally called the submarine, regularly took men on leave to Germany via Nantes, Le Mans, Paris, Bremen and Hamburg. Those who did not leave had at their disposal holiday and rest camps, the « submarine pastures », which were placed near the most popular seaside towns such as La Baule

impressive as they were a tiny majority compared to their Army counterparts. Once on land, the living conditions that were offered to them allowed them to forget a little the monotony and hardships of living at sea. In Lorient, time spent in port was a real rest period for officers, who were installed at the *Beau Séjour* hotel, the same applied for the crew, installed

right
After his arrival at Saint-Nazaire at the end of the summer of 1942, Kapitänleutnant Thurmann of U-553 gives his first impressions to the propaganda service after having being decorated with the Knights Cross of the Iron Cross.
(ECPAD/DAM 1320 L30)

The band was also there to welcome « the most talented amongst them », the « tonnage king », Otto Kretschmer. They play the march that was composed in his honour.
(ECPAD/DAM 864 L27)

or Quiberon, or in the châteaux of the Val de Loire and in alpine resorts. The submariners of U-99 were even sent on holiday to Krumm-huebel in Silesia, the entire holiday being paid for by the Navy ; the men only had to pay for their wives or girlfriends. More modestly, after the official reception, the crew was sent in thirds to recuperate in the villages around Brest and Lorient, before continuing work at the base and loading the submarine with food, fuel, equipment and munitions. Some made the most of this time to get drunk, an attitude which was met with mixed reactions by the Commanders. If the ascetic Kretschmer told them off and promised punishment if caught again, the easy going Schultze, who remained very detached from the rules, preferred to shout into the ears

above
Lorient, back from a patrol, a submarine crew and its commander celebrate their successes in a hullabaloo where military order is openly mocked. The commander goes along with rituals of reversal of values. He is aware that by accepting them on land, at these particular and limited moments, during which the faults and failings of all can be denounced, his authority will not be questioned while on mission, when no criticism can be tolerated.
(ECPAD/DAM 1074 L24)

of hung-over men. Some of the men remained on board to guard the boat. The secrecy surrounding the devices within the boat was such that, in order to avoid enemy spying, no person who was not a member of the crew, even a navy officer from another unit, was allowed on the submarine in the absence of its commander.

They could make the most of this land of milk and honey that was France thanks to the special submariner's bonus. This practically doubled their pay, making them privileged when on land. Some officers were known for their extravagant tastes in Parisian cabarets. Commander Hermann Rasch managed to spend 6,000 marks in one night of Parisian drinking, which amounted to, taking into account the

For the young heroes of the regime, the authorities, led by Admiral Dönitz, wanted to show their appreciation. Along with the bonuses for sea missions were added periods of leave which were veritable holidays, as seen here in the mountains. *(P. de Romanovsky collection)*

Franc/Mark conversion rates put into place by the armistice commission, the equivalent of two years of monthly pay for a French labourer. Without going to such extremes, the men received a package for their leave, commonly called Führerpakete, containing flour, butter, sugar, coffee and sausages that they could take home as a tangible sign of their particular status. This party atmosphere, however, which surrounded the first

above
Although they did not receive the same benefits as their commanders, the submariners were nonetheless pampered by the authorities. When on leave in Paris, no man wanted to miss the shows at the Tabarin.
(ECPAD/DAM 795 L7)

Top left
A 20 Reichsmark banknote. In 1940, one Reichsmark was worth 20 francs.
(Private collection)

left
As with this German soldier guarding an Italian submarine in the port of Venice in October 1943, any one who was not a crew member, even an officer, was not allowed to enter the boat without the commander.
(P. de Romanovsky collection)

previous page
A party in Bordeaux for the men of U-178. In a good natured atmosphere, no doubt for the needs of propaganda, the sailors are directed for one of the reports which glorify, throughout the Reich, the greatness of the submariners. *(DR)*

THE MACHINES

Transmitting

The place taken by transmissions was at the heart of the tactical employment of German submarines. Indeed, despite the repeated requests of Dönitz, the Kriegsmarine would never have an autonomous fleet air arm and the planes that the Luftwaffe allocated were never enough.

However, far from being left to their fate in the middle of the Atlantic, the Commanders operated in combination in sweep operations that covered the presumed paths of convoys. Divided into quadrilaterals, the Atlantic Ocean was covered by U-Boote which the BdU gave, with each new mission, an area to cover. Once a convoy was spotted, an alert message was

successes of the U-Boote, began to fade with the reversals of the summer of 1943. The welcoming of returning U-Boote on the quays, so often photographed, and the receptions, were over more quickly and not as warm. As the months wore on, it was not so much a victor that was celebrated as a survivor. From the end of 1943, submariners were openly advised against trips to Brittany and were told to remain at the base. In order to prevent the spread of information, the *Casino-bar* brothel, which had become the main centre of the Intelligence Service, was forbidden to sailors as well as officers, from now on obliged to go in secret.

right
An invitation for an « party between comrades » at the Moulin de la Galette in Paris, February 26th, 1944. Included is a big raffle ; the invitation card is valid for a glass of wine when presented at the Bunker-Bar...
(J.Y. Nasse collection)

WIE KOMME ICH ZUR "MOULIN DE LA GALETTE" ?

Metro : 1. Richtung Porte de Clichy, aussteigen "CLICHY"
2.   »   Porte de la Chapelle, aussteigen "LAMARCK-CAULAINCOURT"

MOULIN DE LA GALETTE
77-81, RUE LEPIC

Letzte Zugverbindungen : ab Bahnhof Saint-Lazare
nach : Le Vésinet : 23,15 Uhr u. Sonntags 22,50 Uhr
...lles, Maisons-Laffitte usw. : 23,00 Uhr

sent to the BdU, which then transmitted the position of the luckiest submarine to the others which were patrolling in the zone. Contact with Dönitz and his General Staff was permanently maintained thanks to the submarines' capacity to receive radio messages even when submersed at periscope depth. This capacity meant that operations could be guided and led from the central command post. The very large waves, in the 12,000 to 20,000 band, as well as their very great range, were the only ones capable of penetrating water to a depth of a few metres. For normal radio traffic, short waves between 12 and 80 metres were used, distributed according to their qualification in day or night waves.

During the course of the war, because of the lack of submarines present simultaneously on patrol, the number of squares that each unit had to patrol tended to increase, the tight net was thus loosened but the centralized command revealed itself to be extremely efficient. Each unit worked for the others, the number of useless patrols was reduced as much as possible. The Achilles' heel of the system was obviously the number of radio messages that had to be sent, making them vulnerable, due to the ability of radiogoniometric bearings to detect them. Even though he was conscious of this weakness, Dönitz remained certain that radiogoniometrics were not able to give precise enough bearings to be dangerous. Even so, he reacted to this by reducing the transmission time and by transmitting common orders in a

The radio operator, equipped with his three Telefunken transmitters which allowed him to keep in contact with the BdU. Thanks to these he could receive messages on the surface and at a shallow depth (up to 20 metres from 1942).
(ECPAD/DAM 1242 L5)

sages. Thanks to the Enigma machine, more commonly known by German submariners as the « juice extractor », whose possible combinations were incredibly numerous, the Kriegsmarine hoped to confound British intelligence. The way it worked was relatively simple : each key transmitted an electric current which turned three rotors upon which were placed the 26 letters of the alphabet in random order. When the first rotor turned, it moved the second which in turn moved the third, each movement bringing a new letter. The rotors being interchangeable, a considerable number of combinations were possible, the final evolution of the machine had four rotors, five extra

shortened version, thanks to several words preceded by a letter. In this way, reports warning of a contact began by Epsilon, and weather information by WW. This form of protection, however, had its limits when the Allies multiplied their radiogoniometric stations. Thus in 1944, after 45 seconds of transmission, U-66, whilst off the Cape Verde islands, was detected by 26 stations of the Allied network on both sides of the Atlantic, it was located with a precision which allowed surface ships and aircraft to hunt it down and ultimately destroy it.

The second response to the Allied detection consisted of rendering messages unintelligible to the enemy which explains the particular care taken by the Kriegsmarine when encoding mes-

above
The Befehlshaber der U-Boote BdU, or commander of the submarine fleet, was the title used by the Kapitän zur See Dönitz from September 19th, 1939, a title which he kept after attaining the different ranks which led him to the rank of Grossadmiral.
(DR)

right
U-9 returns to Kiel. The commander and the first watch officer stand on the bridge over the circular goniometric aerial.
(ECPAD/DAM 61 L18)

left
The radio operator at his work station, decodes Morse code messages and prepares to decrypt them with the help of an Enigma machine which can be seen in the left foreground. 100,000 examples were made by Chiffrier Maschine Gesellschaft.
(ECPAD/DAM 1100 L25)

previous page
One of the models of headsets used by Kriegsmarine radio operators.
(Coll. particulière)

rotors and 10 different plugs allowing a total of 150 x 1018 combinations.

Theoretically, the traditional means of mathematical analysis and the calculation of probabilities, should have rendered the possibility of decryption almost nil. However, the invention of the Colossus computer would allow information to be processed at a previously unknown speed. Above all, the capture of a machine and its codes in May 1941, on board U-110 commanded by Lemp, by a raiding party of the destroyer *HMS Bulldog*, would give the British an advantage until the end of June, with the radio traffic of the submarines being read like an open book. The different Aegis numbers (surface warships in foreign waters), Tetis (submarines training in the Baltic, Hydra then Triton from February 1942 (submarines on operations) were therefore successively broken.

The precautions taken by the German high command were, however, particularly rigorous. On departing, each U-Boot received its orders and its code for a maximum duration of three months. Apart from the daily modifications, that intervened at exactly midnight in the first months, then at midday, the number changed every month. As well as this, depending on the who would be receiving it, the numbers were doubled or even tripled. There were three types of message according to their content, normal for everyday service and the crew, double coded messages for the officers, and the messages for the Commander. When a message came through, the radio operator passed it to the radio officer who was second watch officer, as the radio operator did not have the codes for deciphering. Normal messages were

above
Fritz-Julius Lemp.
(ECPAD/DAM 1100 L25)

left
Hydrophone operator's trade insignia (acoustic submarine detection). This semi official insignia appeared in 1943. The radio operator carried out this role. His job on board a submarine was of the utmost importance as on his keen sense of hearing depended the rapidity of detecting a propeller, be it that identifying the convoy being looked for, or that of an escort ship in pursuit. Thanks to the 48 microphones installed under the boat's hull, he could generally detect a single ship up to 13 nautical miles and a convoy at more than fifty.
(F. Bachmann collection)

put into the decoding machine and written down in the radio logbook. The Commander would sign them every two hours. Officers' messages, although having gone through the decoding machine, remained scrambled. They would have to be deciphered in a particular way using a system that was known only to the Commander and the radio officer. Finally, the message carrying the title « commander » was immediately given to him who deciphered it by using a grid.

Finally, when Dönitz realised that the Hydra number had been cracked, he hit back by changing, more frequently than before, the range of wavelengths in order to confuse the Allied listening stations, and demanding a more restricted use of radio messages depending on the zones. In an operational zone, the radio had to be used only for the transmission of the most important tactical information upon the Commander's orders or if the enemy already knew the position of the transmitter. On the other hand, when the submarine was in transit or returning to base, it remained possible to transmit messages of lesser importance ; as long as no other U-Boot was nearby.

Even though, from the summer of 1941, the codes were once more changed, and the information on the number written down on soluble paper to avoid being taken if the boat was raided, it was too late. The Allies had managed to find out how it worked, they no longer needed to patiently crack each code in succession, and even when a fourth rotor was added to the machine during the month of

**FRITZ-JULIUS LEMP
(1913-1941)**

Commander Kemp was at the heart of one of the most dramatic episodes of the last conflict's submarine war. At the beginning, whilst he was commander of U-30, he spotted a fast moving ship, zigzagging with all its lights out. Convinced that he was dealing with an armed merchant cruiser, he fired two torpedoes on what turned out to be the passenger ship *Athenia*, upon which 112 passengers drowned. The submarine war against merchant ships began with a drama for which Germany refused to take responsibility, careful to remain within the limits of international law, which if crossed, could result in bringing the United States into the war, going so far as to accuse the British of having sunk it themselves. That is the reason why this sinking was never accepted by the Kriegsmarine. Lemp next won fame for himself during 1939-1940 by sinking 17 ships with U-30, bringing his tonnage sunk to nearly 100,000 tons. However, whilst he was undertaking his first patrol on U-110, the boat was captured east of Cape Farewell on May 9th, 1941, after having been depth charged by Anglo-American destroyers. He was killed in action and was unable to prevent the boarding party from *HMS Bulldog* from getting on his boat and taking the precious Enigma machine, as well as the books used for decoding the messages.

March 1943, leading to a temporary increase in Allied losses, it was outsmarted within a few months. The situation was even more dramatic in that the Allies had increased their goniometric short wave stations, the HF/DF (High Frequency Direction Finder) or Huff Duff, and had managed to understand how the Wolf Packs worked. Once they had detected the shadower submarine, the planes carried by escorting aircraft carriers or land based planes, harassed it, making it stay below the surface so that it would not be able to transmit and continue shadowing the convoy. Once the submarine was submerged, the convoy would make a sudden change in direction, in this way escaping from the Wolf Pack, so that when it arrived in the zone, it found an empty sea.

Hiding from the radars

Radio messages, however, were not the only thing that enabled the detection of U-Boote, submersible vessels that spent most of their time at sea on the surface. With the improvements to radar and the development of the ASV device (Air to Surface Vessel), a radar which was carried by escort vessels then by aircraft, submarines were not invisible as they had been at the beginning of the war. Thanks to this system and the fact that it rotated, the Allies could see in front and on the flanks. Added to this was its ability to see through clouds and in darkness.

The Germans, therefore, concentrated their research in two main directions, concealment and flight. With the first, they sought to perfect the anti radar coating which was split into two types, interference coatings and absorbent coatings. The first Type had an embossed structure made up of parallel surface areas spaced apart by a quarter of the wave length of the

right
A subaltern officer's Schirmmütze with a removable navy blue cloth cover. It was worn from the rank of acting sub lieutenant to lieutenant.
(P-M Rousseau collection)

right
« Death from above ». The planes of the Royal Navy and US Navy relentlessly hunted a discovered submarine.
(IWM)

next page bottom
A U-Boot undergoing repairs. U-67 was one of the first submarines to have its superstructure covered by an Alberich rubberised anti sonar coating. This was made up of 4 mm thick synthetic texture sections (Oppanaol). The results were disappointing and vibration problems appeared. When it left the Baltic where the experiments had been carried out, for Lorient, it lost 60 % of its coating.
(DR)

below
This photograph, probably taken from a propaganda film, is dated 1944. At this stage of the war, there was no reliable way of escaping detection.
(ECPAD/DAM 1100 L25)

enemy radar, which cancelled out the signal transmitted by the Allies. This did not live up to its promise however, because of the difficulty in manufacture and the near impossibility of keeping it in good condition when at sea. The second type was a coating made up of a material which absorbed radar signals and meant that they did not bounce back to the transmitter. Many mixtures were used, an iron powder mixed in dielectric plastic, Perbuna, Oppanol, Alberich (a synthetic rubber stuck to the hull) which sometimes gave good results with a reduction of 70 to 90 % in the intensity of the echoes. This was, however, made too late in the day and did not obtain any significant results.

Although the research that tried to retrieve the invisibility enjoyed at the beginning was a failure, that which aimed at developing devices that detected enemy radar before being detected oneself, proved to be more efficient, even if they were not enough to catch up with the lead gained by the Allies in the field of radar detection. It is true that the equipment which the U-Boote had at their disposal in 1940 was practically nonexistent. They would though, quickly develop a radar detector, Metox-FU (nicknamed on board, the « Nervensäge », literally the nerve saw, because of the continuous sound, resonating within the submarine, caused by the listening of radar transmissions) which, because it was passive, had a range in theory double that of an active radar. The submarine was thus alerted to a transmitting radar well before the latter could get an echo. Even

The American escort aircraft carrier *USS Ranger* took part in the struggle against submarines in liaison with a British task force.
(DITE/USIS)

though this seemed to temporarily reverse the trend, there was a very clear contradiction between the functions of this device and the role of a submarine. The hunter was now the hunted and its only chance of escaping those pursuing it was in crash diving where its fighting capabilities were almost reduced to nil. The difficulty that was posed by the development of new devices was linked to the Germans' ignorance of the enemy radar wavelengths. This was to such an extent that when the Allies began using radar with centimetric wavelengths, whose very short waves allowed for a precise

right
A submarine machine gunned by US Navy carrier borne aircraft. Dönitz described the surprise of the commanders who were attacked at night by four engine aircraft when they though they were safe from attack. « *A searchlight was suddenly lit between 1,000 and 1,200 metres, aimed straight at its target. The bombs fell almost immediately.* » (On average 15 seconds later).
(DITE/USIS)

and long distance locating of a vessel, the Germans stopped, for a while, using the Metox-FU, convinced that the radiations emitted by it revealed the submarine's position. Even if every electric device emits radiation, the detection of the probably very weak radiation of Metox, would have required a veritable high frequency laboratory on board the anti submarine aircraft. Once again, the limitations of the German High Command appear clearly. It is true that the latter did not include any high level electronic engineer and that none ever achieved a rank higher than that of captain. If we add to this the tension induced by the heavy losses and the need to find an appropriate response quickly, it seems surprising that a qualified person was never consulted.

Despite the improvements in German devices, the battle of the wavelengths was lost as early as the summer of 1942. Whilst for two

years, the Allies were trailing behind them in tactical innovations, the Germans, on the other hand, could only follow the progress of Allied devices with responses which were practically obsolete the minute they were put into practice. As the months went on, the detection devices, FuMB (Funk Mess Beobachtung or observation radar) managed to detect shorter and shorter wavelengths. The Metox-FU was replaced by the « Wanze » (bug) from July 1943, an acronym of the abbreviation W-Anz/Wellenanzeiger or wavelength indicator. This meant that the famous « Biscay Cross » was no longer needed (the wooden antenna of the Metox air radar detector) which had to be brought in every time the boat dived, in its place now were more discreet and fixed circular aerials. Although it was simpler to use because of its permanent installations, the latter continued to use the metric 120-180 cm frequency band. It was not until 1943 that it was replaced by Borkum devices then Naxos (the first device capable of detecting the 10 cm waves of the panoramic H2S device, brought into service in the summer of 1943) whose antenna, like the « Biscay Cross », was removable. It was not until

above
This photograph allows one to see the real size of the Naxos detector.
(P-M Rousseau collection)

right
On board U-448. Note the Naxos detector next to the commander.
(P. de Romanovsky collection)

sometimes beneficial to dive and listen out for surface sounds. The ultrasound devices (Echolot) and the micro phonic listening hydrophones were used for both detecting ships without being seen, but also, in the case of attack, to determine, before surfacing, whether or not there were any dangerous escort vessels. However, these devices which were still basic, did not allow for the calculation of the enemy's distance and direction, which ASDIC did. Here we can fully grasp the inadequacy of Dönitz's thinking and more generally that of the U-Boote commanders. All were, in effect, convinced of the superiority of the ingenious tactics and fighting spirit, always thought of as being superior to the capabilities of detection. Even if the will to instil utter confidence in his commanders revealed itself to be effective, it should have been accompanied by an equal intention of developing consistent research programmes in the fight against Allied detection devices.

In warm seas, 1,200 metric ton submarines had a autogiro observation kite which could be dismantled and stored in two water tight boxes on the conning tower; it carried an observer and could reach a height of 300 to 500 metres. On submarines of lesser tonnage, there

the months of April and June 1944, that the « Fliege » (Fly) and the « Mücke » were able to detect, still with a removable antenna, on wavelengths under 10 cm. At the same time, German submarines began to be equipped with the schnorchel which, as it allowed the boat to remain submerged, almost gave back the invisibility of the early days.

Detection was not just for spotting enemy aircraft, but also for finding convoys. Although the sweep method, allied with good intuition and a little luck, had proved itself, it was

...LEIHUNGS-URKUNDE
...rund der Ermächtigung des Oberbefehlshabers der Kriegsmarine verleihe ich dem

Stabsobermaschinisten

H e b e r (Gerhard)

die

U-Boots-Frontspange
in Bronze

Lager 11. 1. 1945
Godenstedt/Ha den

left and right
This decoration instituted on May 15th, 1944, presented here with its certificate, is called the U-Boot-Frontspange (submarine front clasp). It is made of bronzed zinc. It was created in « *recognition of the stubborn and unremitting engagement of the submarines, and courageous character, obstinate and exemplary of their combat.* » The creation of this decoration was necessary, the survivors had had the 1939 war badge for a long time. Posthumous awards were no longer made from November 24th, 1944, the date upon which a second class clasp in silver zinc was made.
(P-M Rousseau collection)

was the more basic solution of the « Wagtail » (Bachstelze) which by using the wind created by the boat's speed, could lift a man using a kite. However, both could only be used in the South Atlantic, which was only lightly covered by aircraft, due to a total lack of defence.

Once spotted, a submarine had no other choice than to dive quickly to a great depth « in the cellar », in order to escape its hunters; a solution which, with the improvements to ASDIC, turned out to be insufficient. The Germans, therefore, developed decoys, destined to fool the enemy about their real itinerary. Faced with the aerial threat, the U-Boot could also release, without having to surface, the « Aphrodite » (a rubber balloon attached with aluminium foils which floated just above the waves) or the floating « Thetis » (which was similar to the hydro-

left
In clear weather, anything goes to help the lookouts observe the horizon. Rather than deploy the cumbersome autogyro, that in the event of an alert would be impossible to fold away and get down, some found it more efficient to climb up a retractable mast, thereby enabling them to see a few hundred metres further on the horizon. *(DR)*

above
These 7 x 50 binoculars, which bear the specific markings of the Kriegsmarine (eagle above a white « M ») were part of a surface vessel's equipment as well as a submarine's.
(P-M Rousseau collection)

graphic floats which had a four metre high mast with metal spines). These radar reflectors, produced an echo similar to that of a conning tower, thus attracting towards them the decoy surveillance vessels and aircraft. Even if the submersed submarine was detected despite these decoys, by the escorts' ASDIC, there remained the solution of releasing a « Bold », made of a chemical composition, it functioned as a protective screen similar to an underwater curtain which produced an echo which for ASDIC, was similar to that of a submarine. Showing its side for detection, the U-Boot would release the « Bold » before turning and getting away whilst the latter remained stationary, attracting the enemy and their depth charges.

right
The « Wagtail » (Bachstelze), was a model of military observation helicopter of the towed autogyro glider type. It was designed and developed by the Focke-Achgelis under the name FA-330. Put into service in 1943 (only on Type IX U-Boote), approximately 200 examples were made.
(IWM)

left
« Aphrodite » decoy system whose aluminium foils were supposed to attract the radars of Allied aircraft.
(Naval Intelligence)

Aiming and firing

The periscope, known by submariners as « the pencil » or « asparagus », played an essential role in the concealment of the boat. There is a difference between the observation periscope and the attack periscope. Before deploying the observation periscope, an initial surface check was carried out with microphonic listening at a depth of 25 metres. If everything appeared quiet, the observation periscope was carefully raised whilst at a depth of 15-20 metres. Its handling was far from simple ; the top had to emerge by only a few centimetres above the surface to avoid being detected, which with the least swell, demanded a level of skill that only experience could give. It allowed for a complete observation of the horizon and even the sky by rotating the mirror to 70°. Using an adjusting wheel, the Commander could magnify objects by 1.5 or 6, whilst being protected from the glare of the sun by different filters. A contax camera or a camera could be attached. When a target was spotted, the attack periscope took

left
The attack periscope of U-458, seriously damaged after a collision.
(P-M Rousseau collection)

right
U-48 returns from a mission bearing the amount of sunk tonnage and its insignia.
(P. de Romanovsky collection)

bottom right
At periscope immersion, the keel of the submarine is a dozen metres below the surface. The attack periscope that we see here only sticks out a few centimetres. *(DR)*

below
In the foreground, the cone from which the attack periscope deploys, in the middle distance, the one for the observation periscope. In this way they were partially protected from the bad conditions of operating in the North Atlantic. They were particularly fragile instruments which needed to be regularly greased and whose head mirrors had to be regularly cleaned.
(ECPAD/DAM 1504 L1)

(for attacks at periscope depth). The angle which was sent to the gyroscope commanding the torpedo's rudder, was calculated by the axis of the submarine's heading and that of the torpedo's path for hitting the target, with all the corrections demanded by the movements of the three mobile elements, which were the target, the submarine and its torpedo.

The torpedoes

The nomenclature of German torpedoes, the famous « eels », is very complex but can be simply reduced two types, even if the variations in the pistol and the guiding system

over. The commander would place himself in the conning tower and position himself in front of the periscope on the leather seat, legs apart and his feet on the pedals which controlled the rotation of the periscope to the left or right, as well as the speed of rotation depending on the pressure applied.

When looking through the periscope there were crosshairs and a replica of the gyroscopic compass. It was far from being merely an observation device. It was a real aiming device linked to the torpedo room which the officer in charge of firing provided with necessary data (speed, distance, target heading, speed and heading of the submarine). The calculator then gave the angle of gyro deviation, automatically transmitted via an electro mechanical circuit to the torpedoes in their tubes, this was done up to launching which was carried out on the bridge (for surface attacks) or the conning tower

are countless. These two main types are in fact developments of the those of the First World War, the G7a and G7e. They were, however, standardised so that they could be launched from submarines and surface vessels (length 7,12 metres, diameter 0,54). They carried

below
A sinking ship in the crosshairs. These photos were taken by adapting a camera to the observation periscope which could also take a cine-camera. *(DR)*

a warhead of approximately 280 kilos of explosive.

The G7a type was a relatively simple weapon, steam propelled by the combustion of alcohol in the air. With a single propeller, it reached a maximum speed of 44 knots and had a range of six kilometres. Its biggest drawback lay in its wake of bubbles, this was solved with the G7e Type. Although it was mostly similar to the previous model, it was propelled by an electric motor and left no wake. The first models had a smaller range of about five kilometres and a maximum speed of only 30 knots, however, later types, carrying more powerful batteries, could reach a target at a distance of 7.5 kilometres. They

Opposite
Loading of a torpedo by barge at the base.
(ECPAD/DAM 1033 L10)

right
A wristwatch bearing the Kriegsmarine initials. It belonged to a petty officer of U-333.
(P-M Rousseau collection)

below
A decorative (and hand made) paper weight. The U-Boot war badge has been attached, curiously it does not have any gild.
(P-M Rousseau collection)

remained, however, less rapid and a hundred kilos heavier.

Far from being simple self-propelled shells, they were veritable miniature submarines whose maintenance was as heavy as it was important. The crew had to remove the torpedoes three quarters out of their tubes every two days, in order to recharge the batteries which had to be a kept at a temperature of 30°, check the adjustments and make sure that the instruments were functioning.

Wartime experience had shown that storing torpedoes for too long prevented them from functioning correctly. Even if this maintenance was exhausting for the crew, it was indispensable in more than one way ; it was not only a

Greasing a torpedo before placing it in the tube.
(ECPAD/DAM 1033 L10)

left
A torpedo is checked before being placed in the tube, the opening of which can be seen.
(ECPAD/DAM 1242 L22)

top right
Cap insignia of U-73.
(P-M Rousseau collection)

following page top
After the torpedo has been completely placed in the tube, the sailor makes the final checks before closing the door.
(ECPAD/DAM 940 L8)

below
As with all submarines at this period, the torpedo launching tubes are numbered I to IV. The even numbers are port, the odd numbers starboard.
(DR)

41, was based on the principal of a magnetic pistol (Magnetischerzündung). They were set to head towards the target at a given depth, a few metres below the ship's keel. When it passed under the hull, the latter's magnetic field set off the magnetic fuse of the pistol. The effect of these torpedoes was greater than percussion torpedoes as water is incompressible and the shockwave covered a larger area.

The problem with this system was that the magnetic fuse had an annoying tendency to go off prematurely, or not at all. Many explanations have been put forward for these faulty torpedoes which was partly due to magnetic interference. The latter could be down to the demagnetisation of hulls carried out on Allied vessels, originally to avoid magnetic mines laid by the Germans in the Western Approaches, or the result of natural magnetic interferences. It was noted that this tendency to fail was higher in the area north of the 62° 30' north parallel, that is, in the Norwegian zone. It seemed that the sensitivity of the torpedo's magnetic charge to the earth's magnetic field was sorely tried as the Norwegian coast was full of iron.

However, mechanical reasons were also put forward to explain these failures, notably due to damage to the firing pin or it being badly set. As well as this, different trials showed that torpedo's running depth was deeper than that which was set. Once more it was the Norwegian theatre which was the main area of these defects. Because of the risk of being attacked by Allied aircraft, submarines were subjected to long periods underwater, sometimes more than 24 hours, which considerably increased the interior pressure. The lack of watertightness of the torpedo tubes led to the disturbance of the devices regulating the torpedo's running depth, the torpedo then descended too deep and went under the target without setting off the pistol.

case of avoiding misses but also premature exploding, the consequences of which could be very heavy. U-39, the first German submarine to be lost during the war on September 14th, 1939, fell victim to the premature explosion of a torpedo, practically as it left the tube, during an attack against the Royal Navy aircraft carrier, the *Ark Royal*.

The first pistols used for torpedoes showed themselves to be a source of problems early on in the war ; this was due to the high proportion of torpedoes whose pistol did not work or not at the right time. The first type of torpedo used was the percussion model (Abstandzündung), inherited from the First World War, activated by contact and much more reliable than the magnetic pistol but whose efficiency was reduced against an escort that presented itself bow first. The second type, which was responsible for the « torpedo crisis » of 1940-

The torpedo has hit right in the middle of the hull. *(DR)*

The second problem to solve for the German submarines was that of controlling the direction of the torpedo once it had left the tube. Early on in the war, guided by their gyroscopes, they went in the direction given at the start which meant that they did not always avoid the destroyers escorting the convoy. Very soon, however, torpedoes were available that could be programmed to follow a course thus avoiding this problem. Some torpedoes were now capable of following a 90° or even 180° curve, which allowed for more attack possibilities. The development of the FaT, (Flächenabsuchenden Torpedo), or torpedo with a twisting trajectory, allowed for an S trajectory through the convoy to its target. It was, however, above all with the LuT (Lagenunabhängiger Torpedo) or bearing independent torpedo, that the number of hits increased.

With this second model, whose trajectory was also sinuous thanks to a gyroscope placed in its head which allowed it to cover a vast area, the angle of the objective was indifferent which avoided the necessity of launching a spread of torpedoes to hit the target. The performance of the acoustic « Zaunkönig » or « Roitelet »

top
Cap insignia of U-333 « Drei Kleine Fische ». *(P-M Rousseau collection)*

below
July 1st, 1940. U-29 has just attacked the Greek ship *Adamastes* **with its deck gun.** *(DR)*

torpedoes, especially developed to be used against escorts, was disappointing. They worked on the principal of acoustic detection and firing (they had acoustic equipment and could, as soon as they picked up the noise of a propeller, change direction and head towards the stern of the target), but were rapidly thwarted by the « Foxer », an acoustic decoy that was towed behind escort vessels, although the later versions, designed to pick up the specific frequency of a ship's propellers met with greater success as an anti escort weapon. Fired from the rear tube, they allowed the submarine to get rid of escorts that were in pursuit. Their rate of success was not high and it has been estimated that only 6 % hit their targets.

Repairs

In the event of damage, the submarine carried equipment for repairs and replacement : an autonomous diving suit, steel putty for plugging small leaks and the equipment necessary for electric welding. The VII C only carried one spare cylinder head but the Type XIV was a true supply boat, carrying cylinder heads, cylinder

AN EXTRACT OF THE MOST IMPORTANT INSTRUCTIONS FROM THE « SUBMARINE COMMANDER'S MANUAL » :

(Navy instructions n° 906)

Title II A torpedo attack when diving

A) Basics for an attack when diving

N° 81. The objective of an attack when diving is to be able to carry out a safe launch whilst hidden and from a short distance. The evaluation of the enemy's speed and position is even more exact when the distance is at its shortest. Launching close up is otherwise more favourable because:

Important mistakes in the factors of firing cannot be of any particular incidence due to the short distance the torpedo has to run.

All of the enemy's defensive measures, for example the changing of heading, if the submarine or the torpedo are spotted, are late.

N° 91. The shortest distance for a close up launch is represented by the distance that the torpedo has to travel at a programmed depth, and by the safe distance for the submarine from the point of impact. It is, therefore, unsafe to launch from less than 300 metres.

N° 94. The enemy listening and detection devices depend, in regards to their efficiency, on the conditions and depth of the sea, the enemy's heading, lookouts and all sorts of other conditions. The danger posed by these listening and detection devices does not constitute a reason for giving up on a deadly attack from a short distance.

N° 105. General rules for an attack

a) Suspicion and caution when sailing as long as the objective has not been found, next, total action for the attack.

b) A thought-out approach as soon as the attack objectives have been found. Continue the attack until total success and destruction with an iron will and wholehearted firmness. During the attack, situations could arise which constitute a reason to let the enemy go. These moments and feelings must be overcome.

c) In war, one is generally further away than one believes, especially at night. One must hold on until the end and get as close as possible. A shorter distance of launching offers more safety for the submarine. When close to its own ships, the escorts will not drop depth charges.

N° 106. All attacks when diving should, in principle, be set up and carried out in such as way as to allow the torpedoes to be launched as quickly as possible. Favourable attack positions can be altered by prevaricating and slowness. The enemy must be attacked as soon as the situation allows it. It is a mistake to leave the enemy behind you and wait until he is within range.

N° 108. Considering the slow speed of a submarine when submerged, it is indispensable that that it places itself in front of its opponent from the beginning of the attack when submerged. The initial position must be reached when the enemy is as far away as possible. In conditions of normal visibility and attack, one must begin to dive for the attack only when the 0°

below
The slide rule was used for the calculation fixed points after observing stars with a sextant.
(F. Bachmann collection)

position is reached in regards to the enemy's general heading.

N° 136. One should absolutely not give up on an attack definitively if one has to dive rapidly to a depth of 20 metres out of fear of escorts or aircraft in the case of an attack on a convoy because the danger exists of being rammed or seen.

Title III A torpedo attack on the surface

a) Basics for surface attack at night

N° 195. As surface torpedo attack can only be carried out at night for a submarine. The aim of the surface attack is, as with the case of a dive attack and for the same reasons of firing technique, to launch without being seen and therefore with complete surprise, from a short distance.

N° 197. d. Important mistakes in estimating the elements of launching are easily made at night. You should get as close as possible even at night, so that even important mistakes in calculation will be of little consequence due to the short distance the torpedo has to run. As well as this, the enemy will not be able to escape the torpedo, even if the submarine is spotted at the moment of attack.

The navigator plots the route for reaching the convoy using a compass and ruler. *(ECPAD/DAM 1081 L12)*

e) The minimum distance of attack at night is also 300 metres.

f) At night one should not fire too soon from a sharp angle. The inexperienced launcher might be tempted to consider the firing angle to be more obtuse than it really is. He must remain calm and not launch too soon.

g) The distance can be easily underestimated at night. Do not let yourself be impressed by the fact that the outline of the objective gets bigger and in consequence do not fire from too far a distance.

1. The danger of being seen.

N° 199. The submarine commander must never lose sight of the fact that his vessel, except in cases of particular unfavourable light, is much less visible at night than a surface ship. A commander's confidence in his own invisibility will grow with each new experience. Any thoughts to the contrary should be banished with this in mind and the knowledge that the attacked enemy is in an inferior defensive position. Furthermore, he is not capable of achieving attentive observation, due to the continuous surveillance throughout a tiring occupation, something which the submarine is capable of achieving at any moment with the highest concentration with an attack in mind.

N° 200. The low visibility of a submarine at night and on the surface is down to its thin and low silhouette as the U-Boot itself almost completely disappears in the water up to the conning tower. This is easily spotted by the enemy when it comes into view on the horizon level with the enemy's view. This is the danger zone when attacking. On the other hand, the conning tower is difficult to see when set against the sea's surface.

2. Favourable attack conditions for remaining invisible.

N° 204. a) Attack the enemy against a clear horizon or against moonlight by appearing against a darkened horizon or on a dark sea surface. The submarine will not be seen, even at a short distance.

c) In all circumstances, it is necessary and right to move towards the enemy with a streamlined silhouette until the torpedoes are launched or the launch position found. The waves of the bow and the stern then merge into one, the favourable position is therefore the attack which begins at a sharp angle compared to the enemy by maintaining ones own thin silhouette by a succession of turning movements (this is what the Germans called a pursuit curve).

N° 210. You should not overestimate in any circumstances, in the event of night attacks, the dangers posed by your opponent's listening defences and for this reason give up on a deadly attack launched from a short distance. (compare with Title II, A, n° 94).

N° 215. The danger posed by the enemy's detection devices should not be overestimated, no more than the danger posed by the

above
For the navigator and perhaps for what seems to be an officer undergoing training, quiet periods could be used to prepare or calculate the position by the stars using this celestial globe and a slide rule. *(ECPAD/DAM 942 L16)*

below
The celestial globe was used to plot the position which would be made with the sextant by establishing beforehand the approximate altitude and azimuth of stars which will be used.
On the globe that we have been able to see are the following markings « Nautische Werkstätten GmbH Kiel » and on an ink stamp « Berlin -Ernst Schotte & Co » « Geogr. artist. Anstalt ».
(P-M Rousseau collection)

listening devices, and must not in any case lead to the abandon of the attack (compare Title II, A, n° 94).

N° 216. One has to expect that many warships are equipped with a surface detection device (DT Gerät: German radar). Suspicion should not, however, lead the commander to give up the attack because he believes himself to be spotted due to an unusual manoeuvre by the enemy or escort ships.

N° 227. The attack itself begins after having reached the required and planned for position in front of the enemy. Concerning this subject, it is advisable to keep to the following essential principle; remain at a sharp angle until the end, maintain, in the face of everything, the « pursuit curve ».

N° 228. When attacking, keep the U-Boot running. Otherwise, the change of surface heading or the crash dive during or after the attack will not be possible quickly enough to escape from the enemy escorts.

N° 229. If contact is established with the enemy escort vessels, try to get away if possible on the surface in order to keep an overall eye on events. On the surface, the submarine commander remains in charge of the situation. If he dives, the U-Boot becomes blind and loses speed, all modifications of the situation depend on the enemy above on the surface.

N° 236. After launching, it will be good, in most cases, to place oneself just after the enemy's stern and to leave the rather dangerous sector as quickly as possible, a sector in which the risk of being rammed is the greatest if the submarine is spotted.

N° 238-239. If diving is necessary in order to escape pursuit, it will be firstly necessary to get away from the area at full speed and in a straight line so that the submarine can escape from observation by the shortest route.

liners, shafts and all the spare parts that it needed to fulfil its role as a supply boat. They were
also equipped with lathes, drills, a tapping
machine as well as carrying 18,000 20 mm
rounds or ten metric tons of munitions. This
meant that submarines could avoid returning
to base if they ran out of ammunition before
running out of fuel.

The U-Boote were used for much longer missions than those planned by the designers and
the essential items needed for the boat's mission (diesel, torpedoes, food, drinking water,
lubricating oil) ended up running out. The
Kriegsmarine's problem was that they had no
overseas port and the possibility of re-supplying
in neutral ports was low, whereas the Royal
Navy could rely on its Dominions for repair and
supply. Although early on in the war, the
Germans used the Spanish ports of Las Palmas
in the Canaries and of Cadiz, they had to give
them up under English pressure in June 1941
due to the illegality of these procedures. The

ingenious system for these submarines was
to slip into a neutral port at night when a
German tanker was present, fill the fuel tanks
and leave immediately.

German submarines could also get help from
surface vessels such as the *Graf Spee* and the
Admiral Scheer. However, after the destruction
of the *Bismarck* and the *Prinz Eugen*, and the
confining of the *Gneisenau* and the *Scharnhorst*
at Brest, the destruction of the various surface
supply ships, whose initial mission was the
re-supplying of surface ships, became top priority for the British. They soon understood that
these ships, positioned in strategic areas, would
see their mission evolve to the re-supplying
of U-Boote. In this way, the *Belchen*, which
was re-supplying U-93, was sunk south east
of Greenland on June 3rd, 1941, whilst the
Gonzenheim, sailing off the Azores, was forced
to scuttle the next day; the same day saw the
capture of the *Gedania* and the *Esso Hamburg*
and the *Egerland* were forced to scuttle.

above
**One of U-333's mechanics
welds, in poor light conditions,
the torn sheeting of the conning
tower after it had been crushed
by the merchant ship it had just
sunk ! The use of overhung
blankets to prevent the light
of the welding from being seen
was common.**
(P-M Rousseau collection)

left
**Whilst waiting for a visit to
the dock in between missions at
Lorient in 1941, a diver comes
to inspect the hull of a submarine
before it goes back to sea.**
(ECPAD/DAM 1098 L7)

right
**A hand made pendant of
U-333's emblem, proba-
bly made on board by
one of the crew.**
(P-M Rousseau collection)

below
**Crew members of U-463
and U-117 are on the
deck to haul aboard the
tow rope to which is
fixed the refuelling
nozzle before diving
and carrying out the
refuelling in safety.** *(DR)*

The technique of re-supplying diesel was basic,
in the case of re-supply by a surface ship, the
supply ship would position itself in front of the
submarine, which it towed by a cable at a speed
of two or three knots whilst a pipeline transferred the precious liquid.

Although the Germans were lucky to get the
Atlantic coast ports, from the summer of 1940,
giving their fleet the fairly safe ports of Lorient,
Brest, La Palice or Bordeaux, the moving of
the theatre of operations to the American coast,
South Atlantic or the Indian Ocean, meant that
the problem returned. The U-Boote could of
course count on each other for help and assistance, notably when one was returning and
came across a brother in arms, whilst he still
had torpedoes or diesel. This solution, however, remained uncertain especially as the
boats had not been designed for this
eventuality, which meant that the Commanders had to show exceptional skill in manoeuvring. The
transferring of surplus torpedoes was in itself a very delicate exercise. Whereas the electric
torpedoes needed a special inflatable dinghy, compressed air torpedoes had to be floated by 18
lifejackets towards the other
boat. The problem of these
transfers was obviously the
extreme vulnerability of the
submarines during the operation.

There remained, finally, the possibility of being re-supplied by the « Milchkuhe » (Milk Cows) which were the Type XIV supply submarines, the first of which was launched in March 1942 to replace the surface supply ships. It was a U-Boot weighing 1,700 metric tons (its only armament consisted of two 37 mm and 20 mm cannons), capable of carrying enough to re-supply four or five Type VII C submarines (500 to 700 metric tons of fuel, spare parts, a doctor, torpedoes, stocks of fresh meat, vegetables, fruits, etc.

Once a meeting point had been arranged, the boats would meet on the surface where the supply boat pulled a 96 metre long tow rope and a telephone cable, held afloat by the diesel pipeline which was filled with air. Once this had been retrieved by the receiving boat (nine minutes for the fastest), the two boats dived to 35 metres, the supplier towing the receiver at a speed of four knots whilst transferring the diesel. In four hours, 80 cubic metres of liquid were transferred from one fuel tank to another. When the operation was finished, the supply boat sent a signal via the telephone cable, and the boats surfaced at the same time. The receiver boat let go the telephone cable, tow rope and the diesel pipeline before immediately disappearing, leaving the « Milk Cow » to pick everything up.

The Achilles' heel of this manoeuvre was that several messages had to be exchanged to arrange or modify the meeting point in the middle of the sea, which increased the chance of detection. Once the source of the transmissions had been pinpointed, the Allies, although they could not always destroy the re-supplied submarine, rarely missed the supply boat which took longer to dive and was insufficiently armed to defend itself.

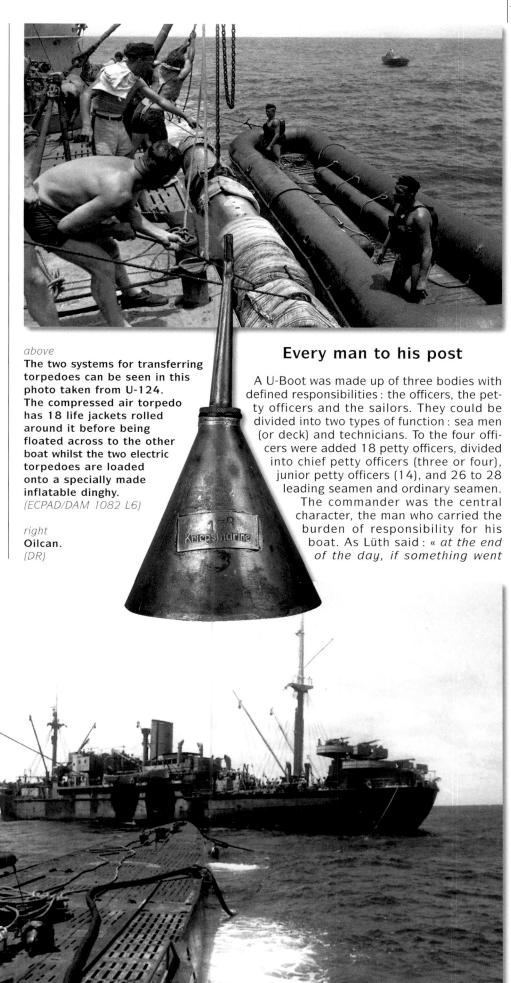

above
The two systems for transferring torpedoes can be seen in this photo taken from U-124. The compressed air torpedo has 18 life jackets rolled around it before being floated across to the other boat whilst the two electric torpedoes are loaded onto a specially made inflatable dinghy.
(ECPAD/DAM 1082 L6)

right
Oilcan.
(DR)

Refuelling by the *Python*... This supply ship was supposed to serve around the Cape of Good Hope with another supply ship, the *Kota Penang*, to supply the submarines. Spotted by the English and under fire from the *Dorsetshire*, it was scuttled on December 1st, 1941.
(ECPAD/DAM 977 L23)

Every man to his post

A U-Boot was made up of three bodies with defined responsibilities : the officers, the petty officers and the sailors. They could be divided into two types of function : sea men (or deck) and technicians. To the four officers were added 18 petty officers, divided into chief petty officers (three or four), junior petty officers (14), and 26 to 28 leading seamen and ordinary seamen.

The commander was the central character, the man who carried the burden of responsibility for his boat. As Lüth said : « *at the end of the day, if something went*

wrong, it was always the fault of the captain and the officers ». The soul of his ship, as Dönitz said, he led the boat and his men which meant that he had to master his own fear and doubts in all circumstances in order to maintain the harmony between everyone and guarantee the survival of each man. Beyond his own charisma, the attitude he had to adopt with regards to his men was far from simple. Halfway between a comrade and a dictator, he had to create for himself a stature as great as the authority he had to display. This necessity explains, if not his distance, at least his reserve in many occasions. In the delicate close alchemy desired by Dönitz, he remained the Commander whose decisions would be contested by no man and who intervened only as a last resort in the internal problems of the crew.

The most important man after the Commander was the LI (Leitender Ingenieur) or Chief, who was the chief mechanic, often with the rank of Oberleutnant. The difference with other navies is that his role was almost the same as

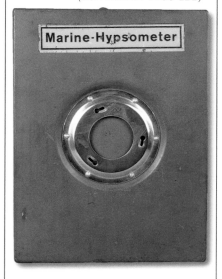

above
Even though a certain joviality was feigned for the needs of the report, it is certain that the relationship between the commander and his officers (seen here « Kaleunt » Peter- Erich « Ali » Cremer and Leitender Ingenieur Spangenberger) was often, if not always excellent, at least cordial. Any open animosity would have been, in any case, a mortal danger.
(DR)

right
In the control room, the starboard side with the wheels which permit the filling of the water tanks on both sides of the boat. The red for the port tank, green for the starboard tank.
(ECPAD/DAM 1188 L22)

Marine-Hypsometer

above
A hypsometer. This instrument was used to indicate the depth by the temperature at which water boiled.
(P-M Rousseau collection)

left
An Oberleutnant Ingenieur on U-124 on his turn to check the diesel engines' compartment.
(ECPAD/DAM 1249 L14)

that of commander reputed to carry the latter on his shoulders. Cooperation between the two had to be that of a good marriage. He was responsible for everything which concerned the propulsion and underwater diving ; the commander also consulted him in all things technical. He had to maintain the boat at the maximum of its manoeuvring capabilities at all depths, something which could turn out to be a difficult exercise with depth charges going off all around. He had, therefore, the responsibility of obtaining from the whole crew the necessary discipline when diving, notably that of silence and the distribution of weight. As with the Commander, he did not have a specific watch but was ready for action at all times, and like the Commander, he had his own logbook in which he wrote down the performance of the machines. With experience, he acquired a sort of special sense that anticipated all the boat's movements. This instinct was not only an optional element that he would have to develop in his specific training but something he

had to acquire. Indeed, once the instruments showed the boat's movements, it was too late to reverse the situation. As a commander said, « Without a competent Chief Engineer, the submarine was a lame duck ». As the nerve centre of the machines, of which he delegated the routine operations to his subordinates, he spent, as did the commander, most of his time in the control room (Zentral). On long patrols, he was sometimes assisted by an apprentice or second engineer who was there to gain experience before joining his first boat.

The commander was assisted by two watch officers who took on a lot of administrative duties. The first watch officer (Erster Wach-Offizier, 1 WO or Eins WO) organized the watches on the bridge and was in charge of the first watch, he made sure that the torpedoes functioned properly as well as the system of control and firing. Guided by the commander, he conducted surface attacks. His role was that of

second officer, capable of taking on the role of commander if needed and that of a go-between for the Commander and his crew, in order that everyone would be on the same wavelength which meant that he identified problems of morale before they happened. The second watch officer (Zweiter Wach-Offizier or II WO), often a Leutnant zur See, was foremost in charge of maintaining the good running of the deck guns and the anti-aircraft armament, as well

above
The first watch officer (U-960) taking the watch on the bridge. In good weather, the horizon was situated, for him and his lookouts, at 6,000 to 7,000 metres, he could, however, see larger ships beyond this depending on their size.
(P-M Rousseau collection)

top right
A variation of the U-Boote war badge, embroidered with yellow thread on a blue cloth backing. This private purchase non regulation manufacture seems to have appeared in 1941. It was not generalised by official instructions, which seems surprising given the difficulty in keeping metal insignia in good condition on board a U-Boot. A very well made woven version was also made at a later date.
(Militaria Magazine)

left
The second watch officer on U-960.
(P-M Rousseau collection)

right
A Kapitänleutnant (« Kaleunt ») shoulder strap, the equivalent of a lieutenant in the Royal Navy.
(F. Bachmann collection)

as supplies and administrative duties. In charge of communications, he supervised the radios and coded and decoded classified messages. He was in charge of the second watch (2 x 4 hours per day). With the cheif mechanic, he shared a post situated in front of the control room, just after the area taken up by the Commanders cabin and the listening devices and radio, which was also the officers' mess where they could talk with the Commander. Very often, the Commander would leave this space to them so that they could criticize his decisions in peace, an essential aspect of the safety valve that officers needed as much as the men. The chief petty officers carried out every day essential duties which were almost identical to those of the officers, who were often younger and less experienced. Although there were four per submarine at the beginning of the war, the lack of qualified personnel made them priority elements and their number dropped to three after 1940 ; they were

either shared out to a greater number of units or they accepted to become officers with the corresponding duties. They shared a small post between the torpedo room and that of the officers, where they ate and slept. In the same way as the officers, they had their own bunk, the only symbol of their status within the submarine. They worked in different parts of the boat in areas which corresponded to the two main functions on board, navigation and technical aspects.

The oldest amongst them was the Obersteuermann (navigator) who was responsible for everything concerning navigation and the boat's stores. It was often a man of experience in his thirties and sometimes the oldest man on the boat. He was generally in charge of the third watch and spent most of his time in the control room where he calculated the boat's position and heading. In the daytime, he calculated the boat's position using a sextant or by using the sky periscope when it was too risky to surface. In bad weather, the position could only be estimated by using the supposed speed

above
An Obersteuermann (navigator).
(ECPAD/DAM 1457 L1 33

right
Although the approach to a convoy and getting away after an attack were more often carried out underwater (especially after the generalisation of radar on escorts), the submarines remained ships which spent most of their time on the surface with activities comparable to any other ship. On board U-103, as with all other U-Boote, an Obersteuermann uses the sextant.
(ECPAD/DAM 966 L16)

of the boat. When convoys were intercepted, he played an essential role, by deciding the best route for interception and helping the captain take up the most advantageous attack position, one which allowed them to fire upon a target again rapidly, or one which gave the most guarantees of getting away quickly.

Also specific to the field of navigation, the Oberbootsman (chief boatswain mate), often called the Number 1, was the busiest man on board. He was in charge of the crews' uniforms and equipment as well as the daily cleaning of the boat. During an attack, he was in the conning tower where he entered various data into the calculator. He was also a sort of mother hen for all the men on board, capable of defusing any conflicts by simply using his authority before they reached the Commander. He was helped by one or two Maat (Bootsmannsmaat) sometimes called Nummer Zwo (and not Zwei so that there was no phonetic confusion with Drei) and Nummer Drei. The Number 2 was responsible for all the boat's munitions and if any was used it had to be signed by him. The Number 3 had to deal with all the sailors' administrative and personal problems, as well as

the last clean up before returning to port. These three men served as lookouts on the bridge.

On the other hand, the boat's technical aspects were taken care of by the remaining two chief petty officers, the diesel chief (Obermaschinist) and the electric chief (Elektro Obermaschinist) who were directly under orders from the chief mechanic, each one being helped by several junior petty officers and one or two sailors. They worked by watches of six hours, although when in the tropics, they dropped to four hours if the chief mechanic gave his authorisation. When the alarm went off, the survival of the crew depended on their ability and speed in transferring the propulsion of the diesels to the electric motors. These men lived in the shadows and only came out to smoke a cigarette

above
Carefully selected by the boatswain, the on board library mixed light works with propaganda texts.
(ECPAD/DAM 905 L30)

or to take a saltwater shower when conditions allowed for it.

What sorely tested their nerves was the necessity in which they regularly found themselves of repairing machines which, despite their solidity, ended up by staggering under

Oberbootsmaat Moskau on the
bridge of U-960.
(P-M Rousseau collection)

could reach more than 55°, with a relative
humidity of 90 %. A six-hour watch in these
conditions was quite a feat and it was not rare
for men to faint in the heat. Even without the
rise in temperature in the southern seas, the
living conditions were made par-

the blows of the conditions they were forced to
work in. Spare parts were not often readily available, and they had to show fantastic powers
of imagination in order to repair damaged
parts. On U-124, they used the foil cigarette
wrapping to make ball bearings for the diesels,
whilst those on U-515, welded two sections of
part of the damaged hull, throwing their guts
up from the fumes given off by the acetylene
welding equipment. Their devotion to duty
sometimes bordered on the heroic, on U-178,
for example, two mechanics used their bodies,
at the risk of being seriously injured, to prevent a piston from piercing the fuel tank.

It was in this part of the boat that the temperatures were the highest. In the tropics, they

above
**Obermaschinist (chief petty
officer engines)
Thieniemann, during a lunch
break on the bridge
of U-960.**
(P-M Rousseau collection)

top right
**Obermaschinist Gerhard
Heber of U-333, his
German Cross in gold
with and its certificate.**
*(P-M Rousseau
collection)*

IM NAMEN DES FÜHRER
VERLEIHE ICH
DEM
Obermaschinisten
Gerhard Heber
DAS DEUTSCHE KREUZ
IN GOLD
BERLIN, DEN 19. Juli 1944
DER OBERBEFEHLSHABER
DER KRIEGSMARINE

Dönitz
Großadmiral

One of the two radio operators (Funkmaat — petty officer) on U-960.
(P-M Rousseau collection)

ticularly hard by the horrible noise of engines that made men temporarily or permanently deaf. To this was added the high exposure to carbon dioxide as well as the constant vibration of the engines which ended up by reducing the men's' level of efficiency and reaction.

The technical aspects of the boat were also taken care of by junior petty officers, radio operators (Funker) comprised of two mates (Oberfunkmaat and the Funkmaat) to whom were attached two sailors with whom they did four-hour watches. Messages could be received at a depth of between 15 and 20 metres and had to be written down even if they were not destined for their boat. The worth of a radioman was measured by the number of messages he had missed during his watch, shown up by the numbering of each message. The radiomen were also at the hydrophones. They were, due to their proximity to the Commander's quarters and their duties, the best informed men of the whole boat, something that they often shared with the crew. They also had the responsibility of playing the records on the submarine in the daytime. With the development of radar, they were also in charge of the radar detectors which increased their workload : this was partially resolved from 1944 by the addition of a fifth radio man.

13th April, 1941. The award ceremony for the Iron Cross for these young submariners. The man with the three badges on his sleeve is a crew branch petty officer (oval insignia with a yellow anchor). Below is sewn the trade insignia of the anti aircraft gun chief, or naval objective for small ships (stylised shell over a chevron). Logically, the last insignia should simply replace that of the same speciality at the base of the sleeve, the chevron indicates a higher qualification than the model without a chevron (basic training).
(ECPAD/DAM 856 L5)

At the helm in the conning tower.
(ECPAD/DAM 1062 L15)

CLOSE UPS OF SOME OF THE SUBMARINE ARM'S SPECIFIC TRADES

13th April, 1941. The award ceremony for the Iron Cross for these young submariners. The man with the two sleeve badges is an engine branch petty officer, who has undergone a basic electro mechanic training called Elektrotechniklehrgang III.
(ECPAD/DAM 856 L4)

Operating the diesel engines.
(ECPAD/DAM 1232 L18)

Once back on land, the men were given leave which was preferable to that of their army comrades on the Eastern Front, exposed to a danger that the men of the Atlantic coast had no idea. This crew branch Matrosen Obergefreiter wears the trade insignia of a Flak gun chief or naval artillery.
(ECPAD/DAM 1049 L13)

A chief petty officer, Obermaschinist, carries out a series of checks on the shafts or an electric motor.
(ECPAD/DAM 1249 L24)

At the front of the boat was the torpedo room (Bugraum), the space of which was shared by twenty sailors and six reserve torpedoes, the maintenance and loading of the latter was the job of a junior petty officer, generally with the rank of second master (Obermechanikersmaat).

During an attack, he would carry out the last adjustments to the torpedoes, something which was originally carried out by a chief petty officer (Obermechaniker or Torpedomechaniker) that the development of the submarine fleet often eliminated. Friction between the latter and the chief mechanic was not uncommon, this was due to the difficult estimation of the water that had entered the tubes of the forward compartment during the launches. What was approximate for one, had to be precise

above
At the dive planes, under the watchful eye of the control room (Zentrale) petty officer.
(ECPAD/DAM 1081 L15)

right
In the engine compartment, a man checks the level of the diesel tanks.
(ECPAD/DAM 1232 L8)

for the other so that he could counterbalance the extra weight by pushing water out of the ballast tanks. Out of the 27 men, there were three petty officers who were in charge of launching the torpedoes, two or three who maintained them, 10 to 13 sailors and 11 to 12 members of the engine personnel who had to make their way through the whole boat for eating and sleeping.

This post was the living area for most of the crew who had to make do with the lack of space. Although those of higher rank were lucky enough to have elevated bunks, new arrivals had to share low bunks which were folded away in the daytime whilst the youngest sailors had to make do with hammocks that were hung in the little remaining free space. Conditions improved a little when the torpe-

CLOSE UPS OF A FEW TASKS SPECIFIC TO THE SUBMARINE ARM

does were launched, the reserve torpedoes were placed in the tubes which allowed the removal of the flooring on which they were placed. However, even after a few weeks at sea, with some of the food supplies gone, conditions remained difficult. The everyday maintenance of the torpedoes alone made this area more of a work place than a rest area, the men's comfort was less important than the maintenance of the machines.

The control room was the nerve centre of the boat that held a certain number of specialists whose particular skills allowed them to be there. Apart from the Commander, the chief mechanic and the navigator who spent most of their time there, there was also a mechanic petty officer (Zentralmaat) who, helped by two sailors (Zentralgaast), was in charge of keeping

above
Controls of the diesel engines.
(ECPAD/DAM 898 L10)

right
Purging the ballasts on U-552.
(ECPAD/DAM 1188 L27)

the submarine's trim when submerged or distributing water to the drain tanks and trim tanks. This mechanic petty officer also looked after the air reserves when diving, the maintenance of the periscopes, and checked the temperature and salinity of the water. When the submarine was submerged, a electrician petty officer looked after the batteries, a helmsman the rudder, and two wheel men (Rüdersgänger) the dive planes to make the boat rise or descend.

In the event of an attack or escape, the dive planes were handed over to Gefechtsrudergänger who were helmsmen who had shown their mastery and their almost instinctive skill in manoeuvring the boat. They were assisted by the chief mechanic, vigilant, with a hand placed on each shoulder. ❐

ROLE OF CREW

Officers (4)		
	1 officer with the rank of captain (Kapitänleutnant — « Kaleunt »)	Commander
	First watch officer. Erster Wach-Offizier, 1 WO (Eins WO) (Oberleutnant)	He was responsible for the organisation of the bridge watch and he took the first 8 hour watch. Oversaw the boat's weapons systems and conducted torpedo aiming during surface attacks.
	Second watch officer Zweiter Wach-Offizier (Leutnant)	He was responsible for the deck flak gun and was in charge of the radio crew. He often encrypted or decrypted radio messages. Took another watch of two times four hours on the bridge.
	1 Mechanic officer (Oberleutnant)	LI : Leitender Ingenieur A highly experienced officer, responsible for the maintenance of the propulsion systems. He also set the demolition charges for scuttling or evacuating the boat.
	There was occasionally a doctor but this was exceptional.	
Chief petty officers (13)		
	Warrant officers (4)	Obersteuermann. Navigation and supplies.
		Oberbootsmann. Crew discipline.
		Obermaschinist. Subordinate to the LI, responsible for the diesels.
		Elektro Obermaschinist. Responsible for the electric motors and batteries, subordinate to the LI.
	Petty officers (9)	5 Maschinenmaat (mechanic)
		2 Funkmaat (radiomen).
		2 Bootsmaat (bosuns, crew supervision, discipline).
Seamen (25)		
		1 Cook.
		2 Mechanikergast (mechanic seamen in the torpedo room).
		2 Funkgast.
		8 Matrose (sailors) without any particular qualifications.
		1 Matrose for the compressors, cooling system and water.
		1 Matrose for the periscope, oxygen, ventilation system.
		1 Matrose for the diving system, setting the ballasts.
		2 Matrose for the right hand diesel.
		2 Matrose for the left hand diesel.
		2 Matrose for the gyroscopic compass and control systems.
		2 Matrose for the batteries.
		1 Matrose for the dive planes that kept the submarine at the correct depth.

BADGES OF RANK: 1 - OFFICERS

2 - CHIEF PETTY OFFICERS

3 - JUNIOR OFFICERS

4 - SEAMEN

1 Captain (Kap. z. S)
2 Commander (Freg. Kap. z. S.)
3 Lieutenant Commander (Korv. Kap. z. S.)
4 Lieutenant (Kap. Leut. z. S.)
5 Sub Lieutenant (Ing. mec., Ober Leut. z. S.)
6 Acting Sub Lieutenant (Leut. z. S.)
7 Warrant Officer 1 (Stabsobersteuermann.)
This here being a navigator.
8 Chief Petty Officer (Bootsmann). This here
being a torpedo mechanic chief petty officer.
9 Warrant Officer 2 (Oberootsmann).
This being here a crew master
(the boss) in charge of discipline.
10 Petty Officer (Obermaat).
11 Petty Officer (more junior) engine
branch.
12 Leading Seaman (Oberstabsgefreiter -
8 years service).
13 Leading Seaman (Stabsgefreiter - 6 years
service).
14 Leading Seaman (Hauptgefreiter)
15 Able Seaman (Obergefreiter)
16 Ordinary Seaman (Gefreiter)

MAIN BRANCH INSIGNIA (CAREER) WORN IN THE SUBMARINE ARM

The yellow coloured trade badges were worn on the sleeve (above the stripes) and on shoulder straps for officers and chief petty officers, on the sleeve for junior officers, inserted into the rank insignia, on the sleeve for leading and able seamen and sailors.

Crew (deck)   **Engines**   **Torpedo mechanic**

This series of illustrations from a period manual shows how trade and branch insignia (career) were worn.

*This un-official insignia was sometimes worn in place of the sextant.

Navigation*   **Radio**

MAIN TRADE INSIGNIA WORN IN THE SUBMARINE ARM

Some examples of red coloured trade insignia worn on the sleeves of leading and able seamen and sailors. The number of chevrons traditionally indicates the more or less high qualification of the wearer. However, this rule was not always respected. Concerning the tra-

de insignia for flak or naval artillery gunners, the second and third chevrons correspond to different qualifications. In this way it was impossible to see a crew member on a submarine wearing this insignia with two or three chevrons corresponding to a qualification in medium or

heavy artillery, inexistent on U-Boote. In the same way, repair divers with only one or two chevrons have this qualification for surface ships « on board diver » (one chevron, or torpedoes (two chevrons).

Diver qualified for repairs and rescue **Artillery gun chief (small vessels)** **Mine warfare**

Hydrophones (regulation model) **Electro-technician**

Torpedo men

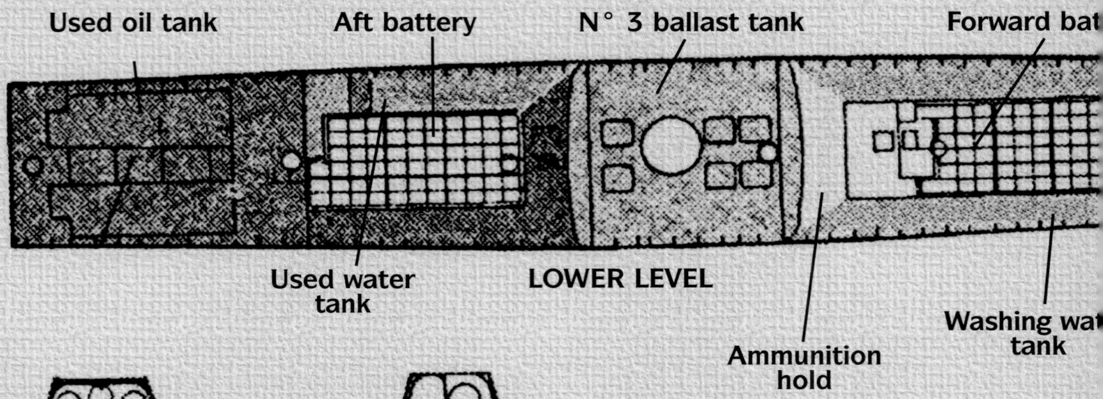

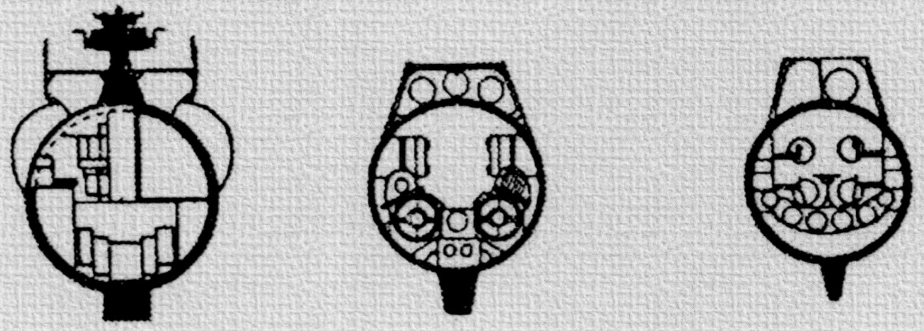

Used oil tank   Aft battery   N° 3 ballast tank   Forward bat

Used water tank   **LOWER LEVEL**

Washing wat tank

Ammunition hold

1 - Torpedo launching tube ;
2 - Crew quarters ;
3 - Reserve torpedoes ;
4 - Heads ;
5 - Chief petty officers' quarters ;
6 - Officers' wardroom ;
7 - Commander's cabin ;
8 - Listening post (hydrophone operator and 2nd watch officer ;
9 - Radio room ;
10 - Forward and aft batteries ;
11 - Bridge and platform ;
12 - Conning tower with the commander at the attack periscope ;

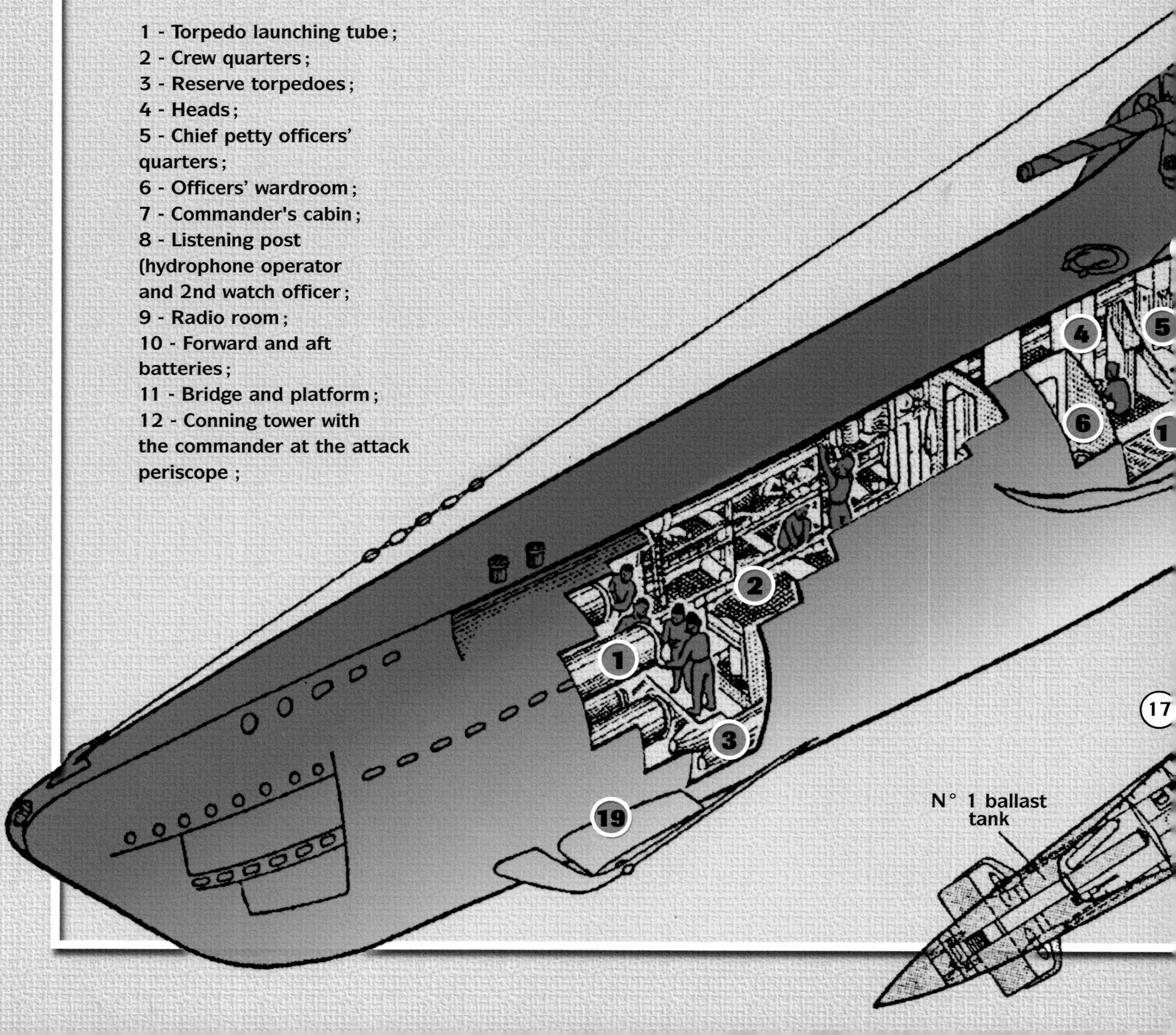

N° 1 ballast tank

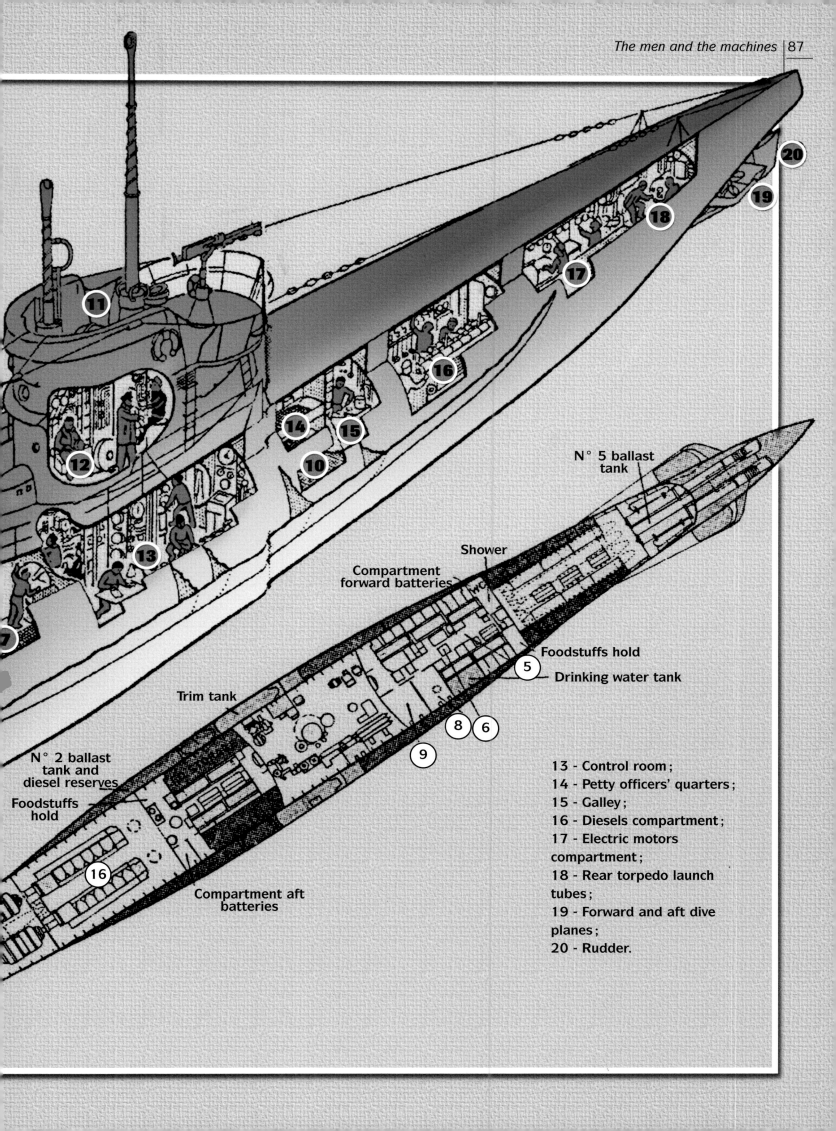

N° 5 ballast tank

Shower

Compartment forward batteries

Foodstuffs hold

Drinking water tank

Trim tank

N° 2 ballast tank and diesel reserves

Foodstuffs hold

Compartment aft batteries

13 - Control room;
14 - Petty officers' quarters;
15 - Galley;
16 - Diesels compartment;
17 - Electric motors compartment;
18 - Rear torpedo launch tubes;
19 - Forward and aft dive planes;
20 - Rudder.

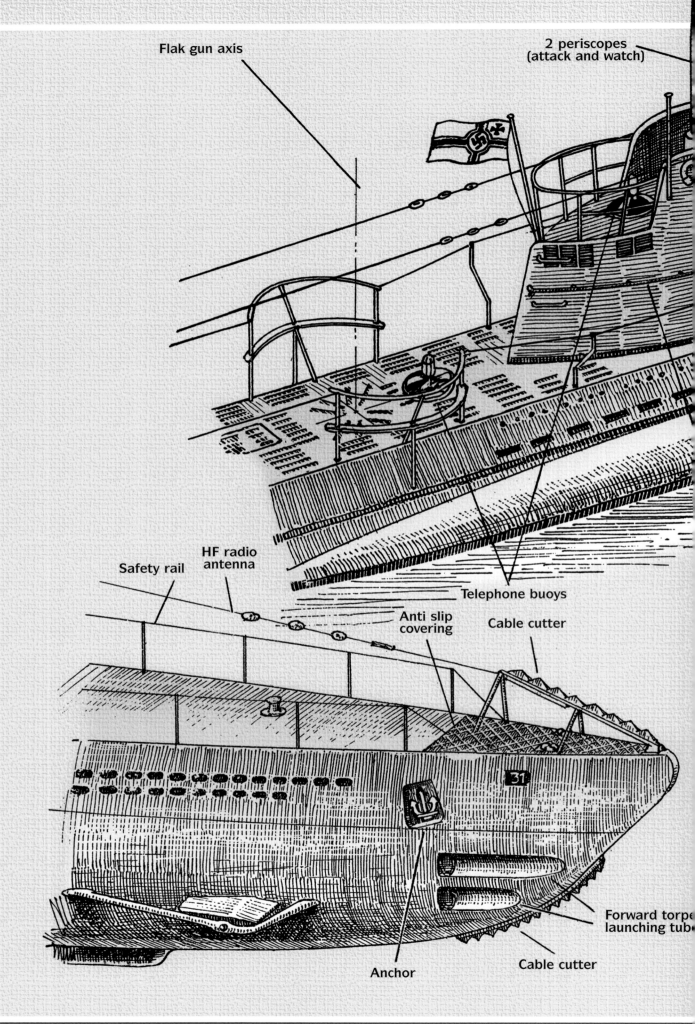

Flak gun axis

2 periscopes
(attack and watch)

Safety rail

HF radio
antenna

Anti slip
covering

Telephone buoys

Cable cutter

31

Forward torpe
launching tub

Anchor

Cable cutter

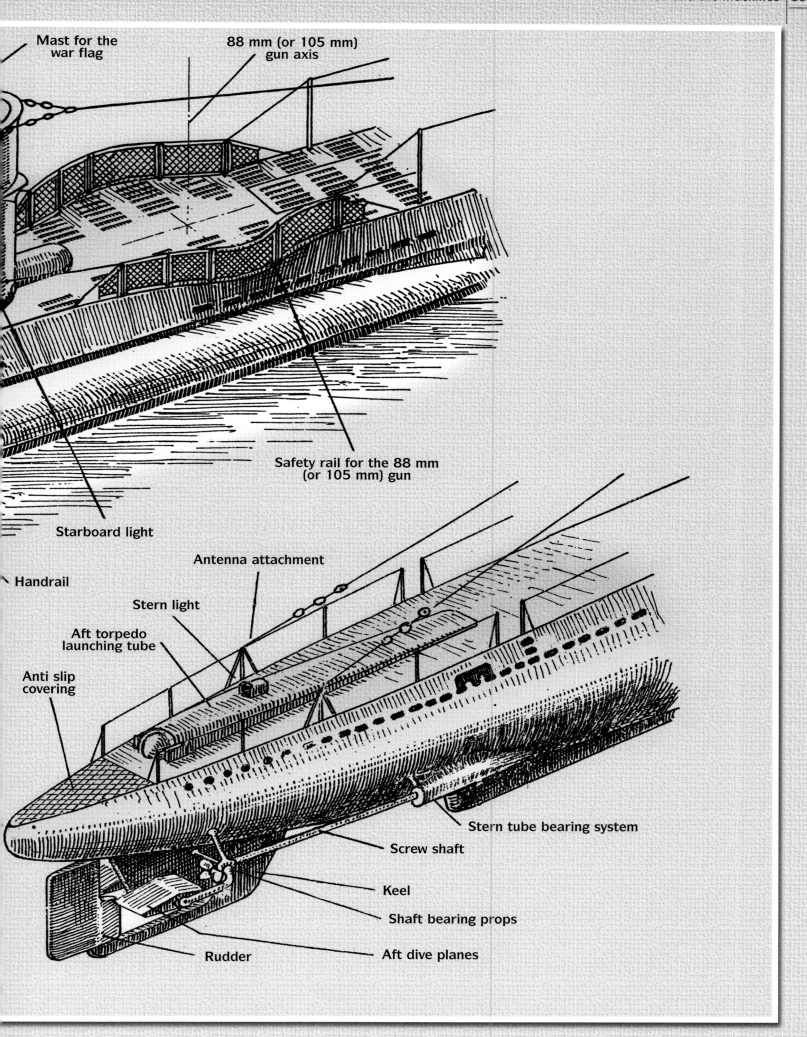

Mast for the
war flag

88 mm (or 105 mm)
gun axis

Safety rail for the 88 mm
(or 105 mm) gun

Starboard light

Handrail

Antenna attachment

Stern light

Aft torpedo
launching tube

Anti slip
covering

Stern tube bearing system

Screw shaft

Keel

Shaft bearing props

Rudder

Aft dive planes

AT SEA

A U-Boot photographed upon
its return from a mission.
(DR)

THE PATROL

When getting under way, the boat was loaded with stores for eight weeks at sea (normal length of time for a patrol), which, if rationed from the outset (which was not the case), meant that they could remain at sea twice as long. The war patrols (Feindfahrt) could indeed be endless. The longest recorded patrol was 100 days, even if the average length calculated from different logbooks did not exceed 36 days.

Torpedoes were loaded last, at the bow deck for the forward torpedoes, thanks to a special hatch, then aft. The operation could be delicate due to the weight of the « eels » and needed to be conducted meticulously to avoid damaging them. The ammunition was loaded next for the 88 mm, 37 mm and 20 mm guns as well as for the machine guns which could be mounted in a few seconds on the outside of the conning tower. Finally, the oxygen bottles were loaded and the filters changed that absorbed the CO_2.

As most of the space was taken up by various equipment, the 15 to 16 metric tons of stores were placed empirically in all available space. After, in order to vary the menus from day to day, an exact plan of storage and stowing was drawn up. The stowing of stores was equally important as a haphazard balance would compromise the overall balance of the boat and effect the navigation when submerged. As well as the importance of balancing the weight, the stores would have to be well tied down so that, when the submarine crash dived, where the boat could reach an angle of 30°, they would not fly around, with the risk of injuring men or

above
Before casting off, the foodstuffs were checked and carefully stowed away in an order that would make sure the crews' menus were varied. *(DR)*

below
The delicate loading of torpedoes was carried out first. *(ECPAD)*

damaging machines. Finally it was important that they did not get in the way when men moved around the boat. Hams and sausages were hung between the torpedo tubes and in the control room whilst fresh meat (for three weeks) was placed in refrigerated compartments, bread, which also had to last a long time, was hung in nets at the bow and in the engine room. It has been estimated that on a Type IX C, that for a three month patrol, the

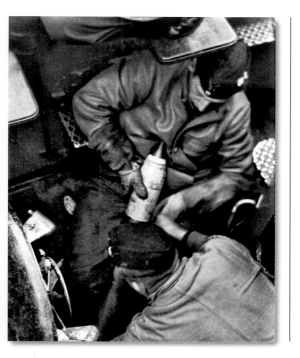

Crew members of U-163 are put to work loading the munitions onto the boat. Apart from the torpedoes, they also had to carefully load 88 mm shells for the deck gun. The number of shells was 300.
(ECPAD)

right
Once the supplies of frozen meat were gone, salted meat made up the essential intake of animal proteins.
(ECPAD/DAM 16L3)

A gauge dismantled from U-123.
(P-M Rousseau collection)

space, which made strong self-discipline particularly necessary.

Food was indeed an essential aspect of life on board as it contributed to the morale of a crew that had to fight against boredom. When a patrol went on and on, the submariners complained of suffering from the « tin illness », an expression which summed up their revulsion of living in a narrow « tin can ». Although food was not the only factor which allowed them to escape this melancholy, it made a big contribution. On board, a typical meal

14 to 15 metric tons of provisions loaded, notably comprised more than 780 litres of milk, 200 of fruit juice, 160 kg of coffee, tea and chocolate powder, as well as 50 kg of chocolate. Once the fresh produce had run out, the crew had to make do with different tinned foods which, in certain cases of interior pressure, could explode, this happened on board U-99, with its tinned duck. This was, of course, the ideal arrangement but a submarine, in the first days of a patrol, actually looked more like a pantry ; all the more so as nothing was locked away because of the lack of suitable storage

above
On U-552, clothes and salted meats were hung in all available spaces.
(ECPAD/DAM 1188 L9)

right
In his 4 m² space, the cook, at his electric stove, had to work magic to prevent the menus from always being the same.
(ECPAD/DAM 898 L12)

below
Cap insignia of the 23rd U-Flotille based at Danzig.
(F. Bachmann collection)

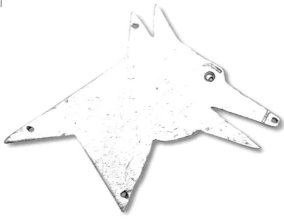

was made up of three fried eggs, sausages and coffee for those on watch. For « Sundays at sea », the cook, in his 4 metre square galley, containing an electric cooker with three or four hobs, a small oven, an electric kettle, a sink, pots and a pan, surpassed himself and made up to three or four different dishes. He doubled the sausage ration, made a dish comprising eggs and cabbage, and served up cheese and tinned fruit with biscuits. He was, therefore, a key member of the crew. As with all the men on the boat, he had a nickname, known by all as « Smutje ». Qualified sailors were known as « Lords », sailors « Tampen-Johnies » or « Decks-Bullen » (deck bulls), a torpedo man was a « mixer », an engine man a « Heizer » (coal trimmer or stoker) and the radio man « Puster » (ventilator).

During difficult periods, the Commander would hand out rations of chocolate with added vitamins. This was all the more necessary during storms, when even the most stubborn cook had to give up, condemning the crew to a diet of cold sandwiches. However, globally, one can safely say that the food on board was acceptable. It must have been as studies that were undertaken in 1942-1943 on a U-Boot crew, revealed that more men gained weight (roughly 4 kg) than those who lost it. On the other hand, if the patrol dragged on in the North Atlantic, where the ability to heat food was reduced to a bare minimum, the proportion was reversed. Alcohol was usually banned on board, even if, on certain boats, stocks of beer were discreetly loaded. On U-68, cold beer was handed out every Saturday. The commander himself took a bottle of strong alcohol on board which could be used as a very efficient anaesthetic if a tooth needed pulling or a limb had to be amputated. Despite the efforts of the cook, the food always smelt of diesel and was often slightly mouldy. Because of the permanent dampness on board, most food-stuffs very quickly became covered by a layer of green mould. After 15 days, if they were not worn, even leather clothing and shoes became green and mouldy. When the bread was put on the table, the mouldy part was cut off and kept to go in

above
To cope with the roll of the boat, the soup bowl has been hung up in the officers' wardroom. Note that the sausage makes up the every day fare. *(ECPAD/DAM 1240 L18)*

the soup in case they spent more time at sea than planned.

Even when rationing was not necessary, the story told about comrades who spent more than four months at sea, having ended up by getting back to port under sail because the engi-

above
Although alcohol was forbidden on board, the officers of U-203 must have thought that beer was in a different category which justified an exception. *(ECPAD/DAM 898 L2)*

left
A vitamin reinforced Scho-ka-kola chocolate box, this was given to men who carried out continuous physical tasks. *(Private collection)*

above
Practice firing but above all in the hope of catching a few careless dolphins to improve the food on board. The men fish with sub machine guns.
(ECPAD/DAM 1064 L40)

top left
The commander of a U-Boot personally negotiates the purchase of fish from a fishing boat in the Baltic.
(P-M Rousseau collection)

left
For U-255 which is operating in the Arctic theatre, notably against the Murmansk convoys which supplied Russia. The harsh weather conditions were sometimes compensated by a surprise catch, here a polar bear which will make a change from the every day sausages and salted meats.
(DR)

left
To make a change, the crew of U-230, lucky enough to be in the warm waters of the South Atlantic, catch sea turtles. The catch is stocked on the deck to make up reserves of fresh meat ; those originally stowed away having been eaten within the first week.
(DR)

previous page top
Cap insignia of U-1007.
(F. Bachmann collection)

previous page bottom
The crew having lunch in the forward quarters.
(DR)

below

Whenever possible, the crew members of U-107, cruising in the waters of the South Atlantic, make the most of the warm water to bathe, joining the necessity of washing with relaxation.
(ECPAD/DAM 1068 L4)

below

A grease pump from a U-Boot.
(F. Bachmann collection)

Opposite

One of the look-outs on the bridge turns his head for the photo, but the look in his eyes shows how he feels about the war correspondant who only sees the nice shot to be had and often knows little about the hardships of life at sea.
(ECPAD/DAM 1186 L21)

below left

Woven shorts insignia (sports clothes).
(F. Bachmann collection)

nes were broken down, and having eaten their shoes down to the leather, made everyone careful. Depending on the climate, the foodstuffs were affected in different ways. Whereas the butter soon became rancid in the North Atlantic, it literally melted in the mess tins in the middle of the Gulf of Mexico where the outside temperature climbed to 40° and much more inside the submarine (which explains why only shorts were worn as a summer uniform), which meant that shaving brushes had to be used to spread it onto the bread. In warm waters, even though life on board was less difficult than in the North Atlantic, it is in any case different from the image of a land of milk and honey seen in photos where the crew is swimming.

Mechanics and torpedo men ended up with eczema caused by the grease and fuel and they had to cover their bodies and faces with iodine, they also suffered from boils.

After casting off, the first baptism was that of the inevitable seasickness, something which represented a real problem as the man suffering from it was temporarily incapable of carrying out his duties. In a boat where every man was needed and had a particular duty, this could have dramatic consequences. The problems posed by seasickness were all the more difficult to deal with in that the North Atlantic storms were of such a violence that no training could prepare the men to cope calmly on a small boat. This was all the more

« The North Atlantic storms were of such violence that no training could enable a man to face them with serenity on a small vessel. »
(P. de Romanovsky collection)

true for the lookouts who had to undertake a four hour watch on the bridge, nicknamed the « bathtub » (on top of the conning tower), swept by crashing waves and the heavy swell.

Until 1943, the real test for the lookouts began when leaving the Gulf of Gascony. When the submarine crossed the 15° longitude west, it sent a last message to the High Command, signalling its position as a Frontboot, a submarine on war patrol. This meridian represented a sort of virtual frontier, after which, keeping a watchful eye was a matter of life and death. This increase in danger was recognised by a combat bonus. Submariners were relatively well off compared to their army comrades as they received several bonuses based on their conditions. In this way they received the Raumbeschränkungszulage (a confined spaces payment), the amount of which depended on rank, for each day spent at sea on a war patrol. Even when they were undergoing periods of training in home waters, they received a dive payment (Tauchzulage), which was paid for each day spent submerged.

Danger, however, did not cease when approaching the French coast during 1943. With the development of Allied radar, aircraft were able to take off from the south of England and attack submarines whilst they were still in the Gulf of Gascony. Despite the anti aircraft guns installed in the « Winter Garden », the platform just behind the bridge, the submarine had to defend itself on the surface against an enemy that was often superior in numbers and whose every hit could sink the boat.

above
U-333, has surfaced in order to charge its batteries. The men form a watch ring to ensure there is no danger to the boat.
(P-M Rousseau collection)

left
20 mm flak gun on the « winter garden ».
(ECPAD/DAM 963 L13)

The lookout ring was made up of four sailors (sometimes two sailors and two trainee midshipmen), a watch officer and a leading rate. Each man had to observe a 90° sector for four continuous hours. They could not warm themselves up by walking as they were attached to the boat by a leather belt which was 10 cm wide and reinforced by steel cable, tied around the waist to prevent the men from being lost overboard. Despite the presence of a watch officer and a man at the front of the conning tower who warned the rear lookouts of the arrival of a wave,

above
One of the various types of glasses with red tinted lenses for night vision. There were other versions with « classic » brown tinted lenses for diurnal vision.
(P-M Rousseau collection)

TYPICAL DAY

00.00 hrs : first third of watch. The starboard engineers watch begins.
04.00 hrs : second third of watch.
05.45 hrs : breakfast for the port engineers watch.
06.00 hrs : crew is woken up, wash, beginning of port engineers watch.
06.30 hrs : breakfast for the crew.
07.00 hrs : tidying and cleaning duties for the personnel not on watch.
08.00 hrs : third third of watch, breakfast for the second third of watch.
08.45 hrs : duties for personnel not on watch.
12.00 hrs : return of the first third of watch and the starboard engineers watch ; main meal for the rest of the crew.
13.00 hrs : duties for personnel not on watch.
16.00 hrs : return of the second third of watch.
17.15 hrs : light dinner for the crew.
18.00 hrs : port engineer watch resumes.
20.00 hrs : return of the third third watch.
21.00 hrs : lights out for personnel not on watch.
23.40 hrs : the first third of watch and the starboard engineers watch wake up and prepare to go on their watch at 00.00 hrs.

the pressure was sometimes so violent that some, never ceasing to scrutinize the horizon through their binoculars, were injured as they were thrown back against the metal sides by the shock. Storms could occasionally hit so suddenly that the men on the bridge did not have time to attach themselves. In October 1941, Kapitänleutnant Herman Rasch of U-124, lost, with the first wave, a complete bridge crew. In such a case, the mission would normally have to be cancelled, it was only maintained because members of the crew volunteered to take over the extra work and Rasch himself accepted to take on a watch.

From the deck, the four lookouts and the watch officer could see up to six nautical miles (12 kilometres) in good weather, but barely a few hundred metres in very bad weather. The problem of the U-Boote was that the importance of invisibility which ruled during its construction, necessitated a very discreet silhouette, with the deck being very low in the water. The low visibility, the waves and the swell had an effect on the submarine's efficiency. When the

right
A crew member on a surface ship has put on his bad weather deck overalls, nicknamed « Micky Maus » for obvious reasons.
(ECPAD/DAM 37 L3)

above
Cap insignia of U-108.
(F. Bachmann collection)

left
« *The storm could hit so suddenly sometimes that the men on the bridge did not have enough time to attach themselves* ». *(P-M. R)*

submarine was lifted by a particularly high wave, it could dive into the next once it had descended into the swell that separated them. With the new wave arriving in the same direction, it was not uncommon for it to pass over the submarine which dived into the depths at full speed due to its steep incline. Apart from the fact that water entered the boat via the two diesel air vents, filling it with hundreds of litres of water that had to be pumped after descending to a depth of 15 to 20 metres, the men on the conning tower went down with the submarine.

In heavy weather, although they were the most disciplined men on board (as mentioned by a French officer, recalling an particularly dramatic encounter between his ship and a submarine : « *not one of the lookouts turned round for a second to look at us* »), the lookouts had an intense fear of facing extreme weather. When the wind was too strong and the storm raging, it was useless to hope to detect the slightest movement of ships or to launch an attack. The watch, in these conditions, was taken by only two lookouts dressed for their watch in water-

above
After diving, the diesel engine exhaust outlets were closed. The small space is obvious here and shows how easily men could be injured, sometimes seriously, in this confined space full of machinery whenever the boat sailed on the surface in bad weather.
(ECPAD/DAM 1191 L30)

proof diving suits, a sort of one piece storm suit nicknamed « Micky-Maus », which covered the man from head to foot and was linked to the control room by a speaking tube, due to the conning tower hatch being closed in order to avoid water entering the boat.

When it was on the surface, the deck watch was made up of an officer and four lookouts for whom the dawn watch was the most dangerous ; this was because the changing light of the morning made it more difficult to make out ships and almost never aircraft. The watch officer was taken from amongst the two watch officers who carried out two four hour watches per day, the two remaining watches were taken by the Obersteuermann (navigator) and the Oberbootsmann (chief boatswain). The dividing of service time into thirds was standard on the

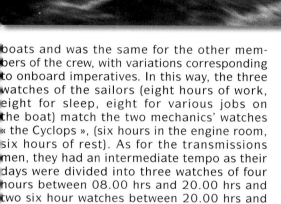

A merchant ship photographed from U-333. It was very difficult to make out ships in the changing morning light.
(P-M Rousseau collection)

boats and was the same for the other members of the crew, with variations corresponding to onboard imperatives. In this way, the three watches of the sailors (eight hours of work, eight for sleep, eight for various jobs on the boat) match the two mechanics' watches « the Cyclops », (six hours in the engine room, six hours of rest). As for the transmissions men, they had an intermediate tempo as their days were divided into three watches of four hours between 08.00 hrs and 20.00 hrs and two six hour watches between 20.00 hrs and 08.00 hrs.

When the time came to change the watch for the lookouts, the man who had finished his service was the first to climb down, the man who replaced him, after taking off the red glasses that he wore in the submarine so that his eyes would get used to the darkness of the night,

left
On watch on the bridge faced with the rising sun.
(P-M Rousseau collection)

top
An issue stopwatch manufactured by Huber.
(P-M Rousseau collection)

left
When weather conditions rendered impossible the taking of bearings from the bridge, or when the submarine had to remain submerged, the navigator (here on U-203), had to carefully note down, apart from the boat's speed, the time that new headings were given in order to reconstitute the route taken since the last bearing.
(ECPAD/DAM 898 L21)

climbed up once the man he was replacing was at the bottom. For the lookouts, a twenty minute overlap could be necessary when taking over a watch, for the eyes to get used to the light conditions. There should never have been an extra man to the normal watch crew for obvious security reasons, apart from the fact that simultaneous changeovers risked being a source of dangerous distraction, a crash dive during an alert could be held up. The four hour watch could thus, for the last lookout to be replaced, be prolonged by half an hour. Once below, it was useless to hope to get warm on the boat. The men were literally frozen, their faces eaten by dermatitis, when they got into their bunks. Even though they had doubled in size (the men on watch put on double the amount of underwear, a training uniform, leather clothes and foul weather rubber trousers nicknamed « kindergarten »), this protective clothing was not enough to guarantee total waterproofing. It would have been, however, out of the question

to have electric heating which would have drained the electricity reserves needed by the engines. Using alcohol to warm up was also out of the question as it was officially banned on board, it would have dangerously slowed down reactions in a world where every second counted (one second, in the event of an alert, corresponded to a descent of more than 3 metres).

For those operating in the Baltic or the North Sea, the situation was hardly enviable, and a long hard stretch of six month nights, watches on the bridge at -25°, and a bow stem that cut its way through the ice. Within minutes, and despite the protective clothing, the lookout was soaked, his fingers and feet frozen and his

above
At the home port, the crew of U-253 make the most of a rest period to hang out to dry their clothes soaked during the mission. *(DR)*

below
A belt buckle issued to Kriegsmarine sailors and petty officers.
(P-M Rousseau collection)

following page
A remembrance booklet honouring the submariners who gave their lives for Germany.
(P. de Romanovsky collection)

beard covered in ice. Although he could hope to warm up in front of an electric radiator installed only in the control room, it took 30 minutes to defreeze before going, half dry, to his bunk at his post. Men, however, had to change their clothes, but after a few days of storms there were not any dry clothes. A new arrival might well be issued with two submariners packs (green work overalls, a leather harness, submarine shoes, two pullovers, six sets of underwear, ironically named « prostitute's lingerie » because of their black colour that hid the grime, and six pairs of socks), but these were soon used up, all the more so as it was formally forbidden to take on board extra clothing which would only fill up more space. A man could not hope to find his clothes of the previous watch dried out, soaked with salt water and in an atmosphere saturated with humidity. One had to be content with, after having got rid of the sea spray with the help of the Navy supplied « Kolibri » eau de cologne, with taking off the boots filled with seawater which were stuck to the feet, and to shake off the salt that covered the clothes. In wartime it was forbidden to get undressed, to be able to face a sudden attack, and the men had to resign themselves to sleeping fully clothed in a bunk with damp blankets smelling of diesel whilst trying not to touch the frozen side of the hull. On the outside, because of the temperature, it was also strongly advised not to touch the hull with bare hands as the skin could stick to the steel. The boat, as well as the men, suffered from the extreme temperatures. They oscillated between -25° and +5° when submerged, and it was not uncommon for the hull to be covered with a 20 cm layer of ice which dangerously weighed down the vessel. The diving planes would not work correctly, the propellers distorted and the ventilation tubes and the ballast tank pur-

In the Arctic Ocean or, as here, in the Baltic the submarine's superstructure became covered in ice, dangerously affecting the weight of the upper areas and therefore the stability. It was, therefore, necessary to scrape off this extra weight before risking a dive which without this measure, could have been risky. *(DR)*

In all cases, rest could not be very long, everyone had to be up for meal times, during which a table was set up and the upper bunks folded back so that the men could sit on the lower ones. As well as this, the sailors' rest was frequently interrupted by the work of adjustment in the torpedo room which involved checking the machines and therefore folding back the bunks. The petty officers' quarters, the U-Raum, was thus called the Leipziger Strasse or Potsdamer Platz, due to the constant coming and going of men (taking over duties, meals...).

Even the pleasure of a cigarette was not possible. Smoking on board was forbidden to avoid an explosion caused by the emission of hydrogen by the batteries, especially after they had been recharged. If by accident, the gas accumulated in part of the boat, the slightest spark could set off an explosion. Smoking was therefore only possible on the surface within a given timetable and only by one or two men at the same time to avoid overcrowding the brid-

ges risked being blocked at any moment, something which would have prevented a rapid dive.

In any case, it was difficult to get proper rest. The noise of the submarine's engines prevented all rest with their steady thumping which was accentuated by the long metal cylinder of the submarine which acted as a resonance chamber. Added to this permanent heavy noise were the ventilators which ended along the conning tower. Even those at rest could not sleep until the time of their watch. The boat could roll in heavy weather, on the surface, to an extent and a force much superior to that of a conventional vessel. Rolling at 30° was common and those at sleep could find themselves thrown out of their bunk, despite the protective board, and find themselves in the lower bunk on the opposite side. For those who had given up on sleep, the sitting position was hardly any more comfortable, due to a lack of head height. Moreover, all of the forward post was lacking in height, because as long as there were reserve torpedoes, the men walked on a false floor which prevented them from being able to stand up completely.

top
On board U-458, the sailors in charge of the diesels tune the engines. The noise emitted by the latter, but also by the ventilators which worked at full power, the boat being necessarily on the surface, made work conditions very harsh. *(DR)*

above
The sailors' rest periods were often interrupted by the maintenance in the torpedo room.
(DR)

left
Behind the control room, the petty officers' quarters gave access to the engine compartments. Despite the apparent calm, it was regularly passed through by men coming from the forward post before taking their watch post at the diesel or electric engines.
(DR)

4.40 45 deutsche U=Boot=Fahrer erzählen Kriegserlebnisse

Was all diese berühmten Kommandanten und Offiziere, diese schlichten Matrosen und Maschinisten an schneidigen Taten, kühnen Abenteuern und eiserner Pflichterfüllung berichten, Seite um Seite fesselt es den Leser immer von neuem. Ein unerhörtes Geschehen hält ihn in atemloser Spannung und lä...

ge which was already occupied by the lookouts. To avoid errors, the smokers had to wait their turn and signal their presence outside by a peg that they stuck to a panel in the conning tower or by a single ring, marked « R », for Raucher (smoker) that they wore around their neck. This moment of relaxation was only possible in the daytime as the smallest point of light was visible from a great distance in the very pure night air. In bad weather, smoking in this way was quite simply unthinkable. Some, however, did not hesitate in breaking this rule, at the risk of severe punishment if caught. It was difficult though to carry out a punishment in an environment where it was impossible to isolate, lock up, or *a fortiori* disembark any man. The only solution was to therefore reprimand the offender and make him sign a promise that made him

following page
A packet of Gute Privat cigarettes.
(Private collection)

right
A Leutnant's cross over jacket and his leather coat, condemned to remain damp due to the lack of heating. *(ECPAD)*

behave in a better way if he did not want to be punished on his return.

Even when the sailing conditions were better, they remained tough. Apart from the interior humidity which was difficult to put up with, the mouldy food and clothes, the air which was breathed smelt of diesel, cooking and 50 men who did not wash very often. They could only use a little fresh water once a day in the morning to clean their teeth, when possible. On the other hand, for washing their bodies, they used a little sea water with soap specially made to froth up with salt water. However, few used it regularly as it left a film on the skin, even if it meant catching body lice quickly. Added to

above
In front of the reporter's camera, the men equipped with their life jacket can at last have their midday cigarette.
(Private collection)

top
Cap insignia of U-205.
(P. de Romanovsky collection)

left
Washing. Fresh water, something which was just as precious as fuel or torpedoes, was rationed for the men who had to make do with the bare minimum.
(ECPAD/DAM 1248 L21)

right
The famous heads, the use of which soon became a nightmare for the men. Note to the right of the bowl the pump which was soon unusable at a great depth and which in any case needed great strength.
(ECPAD/DAM 1187 L22)

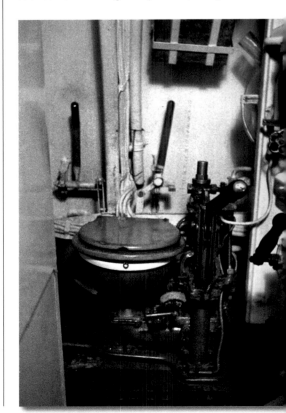

On the surface, when weather and tactical conditions allowed it, the men (here on U-103), preferred to use the chair with the hole rather than the uncomfortable heads on board.
(ECPAD/DAM 965 L8)

this was the stench of the latrines, regularly unusable, which was enough to make the toughest of sailors feel ill. The crew only had two toilets for fifty men, one of which was unusable during the first half of the voyage as it was used for storing food. The other was, therefore, heavily used. Using them was a real trial. Indeed, a submarine, when submerged, was like a balanced weight, and every man who left his post compromised the balance. He had to

below
When resupplying, the men could make the most of the *Kormoran*'s fresh water tanks to get rid of the awful suffocating smell that pervaded the interior of the submarine.
(ECPAD/DAM 1082 L21)

ask the control room chief permission to go. To avoid unnecessary movement from fore to aft, small red lights were lit to indicate whether the toilets were in use. After managing to get into this place no less comfortable given its size (0.50 x 0.50 metres), it was difficult to stay there for long as comrades demanded to go or an alert meant going back to one's post. As for using the toilet at a great depth, it was pointless, given that pulling the flush

required out of the ordinary strength, the pumps, at least until 1944, were not powerful enough to fight the external pressure at a depth of 25-30 metres. As well as this, the bowls were more often made of porcelain which made them very fragile. A large number of bowls were broken by the shockwaves of explosions. And woe betide the man who did not know how to flush out the dirty water : the shower made up of the contents of the bowl mixed with seawater was the immediate penalty for

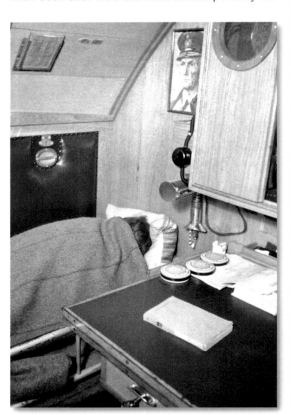

above
A petty officer of the engines branch plays a board game. Note the folded bunk. On board any space was precious and when the bunks were set up in the forward compartment, the men only had enough space to lie down.
(ECPAD/DAM 1100 L20)

top right
Some men used their free time to make objects, models of their boat with the help of the milling machine, copies of decorations or the U-Boote war badge made with a file and as seen here, a personalised box bearing the symbol of their submarine.
(Private collection)

right
In the forward compartment, the lack of available bunks, with some used to hold foodstuffs at the beginning of a patrol, meant that the last men to arrive had to sleep in hammocks which at least saved them from the falls caused by the boat's roll.
(ECPAD/DAM 1256 L20)

left
The commander's cabin on U-552, is as spartan as all commanders' cabins on U-Boote were. Note the three metal boxes of vitamin reinforced Scho-ka-kola chocolate.
(ECPAD/DAM 1188 L16)

his lack of concentration. U-1206, commanded by Kapitänleutnant Schlitt, was lost on April 13th, 1945, after a dysfunction with the toilets : as seawater flooded into the submarine, the hydrochloric acid fumes given off by the water coming into contact with the batteries, meant that the submarine had to surface. As it was very close to the coast of Northern Scotland, it was immediately noticed by Allied aircraft and sunk within a few minutes.

More than this foul smell, which was cleaned up as quickly as possible when returning to port, as the submariners associated it with death and it put off the technical teams, it was the absence of night and day, life regulated by

watches that wore the men down as much as the lack of sleep and the smell. Added to this was the utter lack of privacy, the impossibility of being alone and having to share one's bunk with one's neighbour, which ended up affecting everyone's morale. Although the professional sailors shared two bunks for three, the other crew members shared between them the 12 bunks of the torpedo room. Only the men responsible for launching torpedoes, the radio men as well as technical or mechanical personnel had their own bunk or one for two men.

This insidious torpor, broken only by meal times, had to be fought against by the commander who found things to keep the men occupied by celebrating feast days and Sunday or by celebrating birthdays for which the cook would make the favourite food of the man whose birthday it was. The most enterprising commanders, notably Lüth, went so far as to organise competitions of singing, chess, skat (a sort of card game) or poetry. When a submarine spent Christmas at sea, the first watch officer would bring presents for everyone, Commander Hardegan, in December 1941, went so far as to bring on board a Christmas tree with electric lights. As an ex-submariner, conscious of the hardships of this existence cut off from the world, Dönitz himself did not hesitate, when it was still possible, to break radio silence to announce a birth with a code which became famous : « *a submarine with periscope arrived today* », for a boy, « *without periscope* » for a girl.

Despite these arrangements, circumstances often made men make sacrifices which, as the patrol went on, became very difficult to accept. Operations that approached the coasts, which meant remaining under water for 14 or even 16 hours, were particularly dreaded by the Commanders. The air rapidly became polluted, even more so as the men moved about more, everything possible was done to prevent

right
A game of cards. The circular openings through the bulkheads, which allowed men to get from one compartment of the boat to another were equipped with watertight doors that could be used to cut off a flooded part of the boat. *(DR)*

below
In the officers' wardroom, as elsewhere on the boat, games could help kill the endless hours of waiting.
(ECPAD/DAM 942 L14)

the crew from tiring too quickly ; this meant that work and movement had to be reduced to a minimum. When the boat was under water (which became more frequent with the arrival of the schnorchel), activity was limited to save oxygen. Commanders were the first to encourage their men to go to their bunks and sleep, with the exception of the chief mechanic who

had to show all his skill in keeping the boat at the correct depth.

To avoid cooking smells and to save electricity, the men ate cold meals when submerged and the meals were reversed, that of midday (dinner in the navy) was eaten at night when the U-Boat sailed on the surface. Long dives which allowed the schnorchel posed new problems which had to be solved in order to avoid the already difficult conditions caused by closed spaces from worsening. The need to get rid of waste also came to the fore when it was impossible to surface for throw away the rubbish. The solution adopted was found by placing the waste in the torpedo tube and to fire it out, this was nicknamed the « Müllschuss » (firing of rubbish). This was carried out twice a week. Although this allowed for rubbish to be got rid of, the smell that it gave off in the torpedo room remained.

Despite these precautions, air pollution was inevitable in a diving submarine. Different substances were permanently suspended in the air. Tests were therefore carried out by the Germans, notably when the schnorchel was installed in the U-Boote, to determine the consequences and the thresholds of these gases. The commission of Doctor Cauer, nicknamed « Doctor Pollution », therefore tried to determine the substances which were present and the thresholds that they reached in the different posts. In first place was ammonia,

above
The cook, who shared the same dangers as the rest of the crew, allows himself some respite. Note behind him one of the boat's ten loudspeakers.
(ECPAD/DAM 1100 L22)

left
This Bordmütze bears the insignia of the 1st U-Flotille, the ex-Weddingen flotilla in peacetime. It operated out of Brest from June 1941 to September 1944.
(P-M Rousseau collection)

below
Time spent on the surface was used to get rid of rubbish that when submerged, took up space and stank.
(ECPAD/DAM 965 L9)

the consequences of which could be deadly. In fresh air there were eight units, in the smoke of burning leaves and wood 675, quantities measured in the engine room revealed more than 550 units and up to 600 in the galley. In the engine room, when sailing with the schnorchel, this could vary between 10,000 and 15,000 units during two steam jets. These are of course only quantities calculated from found ammonia matter and not free ammonia but no one knows if, over a long period, these quantities did not have an adverse biological effect on the body. The amount of nitrates was just as high. This combination, similar to nitrogen, could pass the poison threshold when the engines were pushed. Formaldehyde caused cramps from 350 units in the air and doses comprised between 0,1 and 905,6 units were calculated whilst the average values in the electric motor room were 40 units, 150 units in the engine room and 60 in the petty officers' mess and post. When sai-

left

Ernst Beinert and Walter Schöckel of U-103, both wearing their leather trousers, get some rest in the forward compartment, not only due to the fatigue of their watch but also because they were strongly advised to lie down in order to diminish the 20 litres of carbonic acid produced every hour by their lungs.
(ECPAD/DAM 1062 L1)

accidents which resulted in death, such as that of Kapitänleutnant Rolf Mützelberg, commander of U-203, who broke his neck when jumping into the water where his crew were swimming off the Azores, « industrial accidents » were much more frequent.

Although the latter could cause wounds which were long to heal in a confined and damp environment, it was infectious and venereal diseases (crabs, scabies) which constantly appeared. This was the reason why many submarine crews underwent a week of health treat-

above

The noxious fumes, mixed with the smell of food, oils and sweat made the ventilation of the boat essential.
(ECPAD/DAM 1042 L22)

ling with the schnorchel, during steam jets, 300 to 15,000 units were recorded and up to 60,000 units near the pressure valves.

Mixing the air of the submarine was, therefore, indispensable. Ventilators circulated the air in the submarine and pushed it over sets of potassium cartridges which, by chemical reaction, kept the carbonic acid and released oxygen. But, despite this precaution, the first trials of the schnorchel caused accidents. Comprising a double tube of 7.80 metres, closed by two floating valves, one pulling in the air for the engines, the other pushing out the exhaust fumes, this system could, when used incorrectly, turn out to be dangerous. If it remained under water, the engines suffocated and stopped, but not without having pumped out the air inside the submarine, creating a sudden depressurisation of around 400 to 500 millibars (equivalent to a difference in altitude of 0 to 4,000 metres). Crews were subjected to head and tooth aches, whilst the eardrums could suddenly burst, from 450 millibars, men could begin to blackout. The tests carried out showed that only a quarter of the crews having sailed for a long time with the schnorchel conserved their original hearing capacities.

Accidents were even more difficult to deal with as the majority of U-Boote could not take on board doctors (only the Type X B minelayers and Type XIV supply boats, as well as the Type IX S sailing in the Indian Ocean carried a Stabarzt). They had to make do with first aid carried out by one of the leading rates who had been trained for it. With the best will in the world, some cases sometimes needed a real doctor which meant transferring the wounded onto another submarine that carried a doctor, or one which was returning to base. Although

ment at Carnac ; this was an integral part of their preparation for the next patrol. It was in this area that the naval institute of medical research for U-Boote (Marineärztliches Forschungsinstitut für Ubootmedezin) was established between January 1942 and August 1944.

right

Shoulder straps of an acting sub lieutenant's and a Fänhrich, both are of the engines branch.
(F. Bachmann collection)

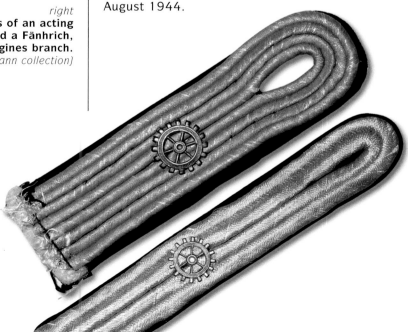

COMBAT POST

Waiting, which represented most of the time spent on patrol, was in itself a particularly trying test on the nerves as men had to remain on permanent alert, which ended up leading to nervous breakdowns. Conscious of this aspect of life on board, the navy high command, at the beginning of the war, took the sailors away from the frontline who had accomplished 12 war patrols, whether or not they wanted to. Although this measure remained in vigour until the end of the war, it was hardly ever put into practice from 1943 as not many men could boast of such a record. Of the 40,000 German submariners, more then three quarters never came back.

The tension that was the result of waiting was often so hard to live with, that an alert, despite the danger of death which it represented, ended up being a sort of relief. When an escort was detected, the watch officer, equipped with a compass, a transmitter for orders (then, a microphone at the end of the

above

It was rare to have a doctor on board. This was, however, the case at the end of September 1941 for U-68. After having victoriously attacked a convoy with three other brothers in arms, including U-67, Stabarzt Ziemke boarded the latter to check over a crew member who had caught a venereal disease. Not able to do anything with this case, he had the man put on U-68 which was heading back to France. On a day to day basis, it was often a petty officer with a few basic notions and a first aid kit who dealt with medical cases.
(ECPAD/DAM 1062 L1)

above
Sleeve insignia of the medical branch.
(F. Bachmann collection)

left
Before setting off the men had to have a medical.
(ECPAD/DAM 1072 L30)

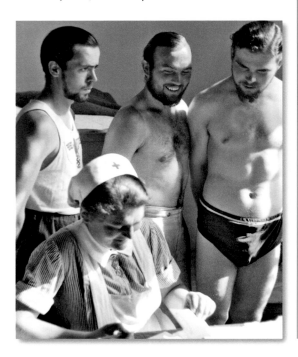

year) and an alert button, sounded the alarm. The two switches were placed side by side, the first for diving and the second for an air alert. The role of the watch officer was therefore decisive as, depending on the distance of the aircraft, he had to decide whether to dive or fight back with the anti aircraft guns (Flak). If the aircraft was far away, he pressed the dive switch ; however from a short distance, diving would have been suicidal as the plane could have been over the submarine before it could be completely underwater and therefore powerless and a perfect target.

The solution, that the Germans thought they had come up with, was based on a powerful anti aircraft defence with a group of at least three submarines that escorted their comrades until they reached the free waters of the Atlantic.

This defence, however, was quickly turned out to be useless against planes which were happy to observe the submarines from a distance enough to escape the German guns. From this altitude, they called for air or maritime reinforcements when they were at the limit of their range. Submarines were therefore caught in a trap, not being able to dive or wait indefinitely. The only solution would have been to carry guns capable of pushing the planes back far enough, giving the submarines time to dive. The men on the bridge would jump into the conning tower, the last

man closing the second watertight hatch which sealed the conning tower. The crew's survival depended on the rapid reactions of the men on the bridge who carried out a drill that had been practised a thousand times over. The leather harness that held them to the bridge was cut with an axe, and the men jumped one after the other through the hatch. In particularly perilous situations, some men did not have enough time to get out of their leather harness and went down with the submarine. For them, if it was not a false alert, or if circumstances did not allow to re-surface immediately, it was certain death. The case of chief helmsman Gustav Krieg, nicknamed « Der druckfeste Gustav » (Gustav the pressure) is exceptional. During a crash dive, the latter did not have enough time to release the hook which held him to the rail of U-269 commanded by Uhl, and remained attached by a rope. When Uhl finally realised, the unlucky man was recovered, fainted, but alive, he had been down to a depth of 45 metres !

During training exercises, which could not exceed five seconds until the hatch was closed, the men gave up on descending the ladder normally and made do with placing their hands and feet on the rail before sliding down into the interior. When they were at the bottom, they had to immediately move to one side, sometimes helped by a sailor who pulled them away so that the next man with his heavy boots

above
Dusk falling on the sea was for submariners, if a convoy had been spotted, the advent of combat.
(ECPAD/DAM 1186 L3)

top right
7 x 50 binoculars made by the famous optical manufacturer Carl Zeiss (Jena). This « U-Bootglass » was introduced in 1943 for the use of submariners.
(P-M Rousseau collection)

left
**« *The answer that the Germans had thought they had found for their problems rested on a strong anti aircraft defence.* »
Illustration by Tress.**
(ECPAD/DAM 1515 L3)

right
The lookouts peer down the conning tower ladder. Note the narrow passage that the five men on the bridge will have to descend in less than 20 seconds if the alert is given.
(ECPAD/DAM 1062 L24)

would not land on their head. The last man to jump down was the watch officer who, to gain a few seconds, jumped into the conning tower whilst holding the hatch so that it would close as he jumped. When he was hanging from the hatch, his legs in the air, he would shout « *dive !* ». However, faced with immediate danger, it was not rare for the watch officer to order the dive whilst he was still above and the hatch open.

Once the alarm horn was sounded, the diesels shut down and with the closure of the air vents in the engine room, the two electric powered propellers were activated. To achieve a total synchronicity, the exercise was repeated many times so that it became automatic. For those who forgot something, the slightest oversight was given away by a red light which came on immediately. At the same time, the order to dive had barely been given that the engineer mechanic ordered the air of the ballasts to be purged as soon as he judged the

above
**Some of the crew members
of U-552 in the control room.**
(ECPAD/DAM 1185 L3)

left
**« *Alert !* » (illustration by Tress).
The crash dive procedure was
called « Stuka Tauchen ». Barely
conforming to regulations,
it comprised particularly
precise orders and movements.**
(ECPAD/DAM 1515 L1)

At the same time, the electric motors were at full power so that maximum depth could be reached as fast as possible. Once at 20 metres, the chief mechanic announced to the commander that the « *the dive tanks were open* ». At the same time he had to flush out the five metric tons of water necessary for sailing at periscope depth (which now dangerously weighed down the submarine), allowing the counterbalancing of the « surface attraction » and to hasten the dive. Upon his order, the compressed air, stocked at 205 kg,

vessel ready to dive. When the submarine was barely able to float, and the ballast tanks half full, it could dive in less than 20 seconds by opening the air purges. In front of the engineer mechanic was a panel of lights which indicated the level of the five ballast tanks. The first to open was door n° 5 and it was followed by the next three which were placed in pairs, port and starboard.

When the indicator lights of the first four ballast tanks lit up simultaneously, indicating their opening, the water flooded in and made the boat dip at 10° then 20°. It was only when this angle was achieved that the chief mechanic finally ordered the opening of the aft ballast tank n° 1, which was the last to be opened in order to accelerate the submarine's angle so that it would dive more quickly.

above and right
**An award certificate accompanying
an Iron Cross 1st Class. This is
the first type, printed in gothic
script. It was awarded on
February 10th, 1942 to a
submariner.** *(P-M Rousseau coll.)*

Im Namen des führers
und Obersten Befehlshabers
der Wehrmacht
verleihe ich
dem
Obermaschinisten
Gerhard Heber
das
Eiserne Kreuz 2. Klasse
Befehlsstelle....., den 10. Februar 194...

me when sailing under water. If, at a great depth, the air compressed and weighed down the vessel, at an average depth, air bubbles would get stuck fore or aft, depending on the boat's angle, and unbalance it.

During this time, the dive, decided by the watch officer, was in the hands of the technicians. When the boat was safe for a while, the watch officer would tell the commander why he decided to dive (it should be realised that with a plane flying at an altitude of 4,000 metres, if it was not in the right direction, the submarine would already be 50 metres under water before it could drop its depth charges). Immediately after, the engineer mechanic would give the commander a report on the situation comprising the depth, depth speed and angle of the boat. It was only when he had received this data that the commander took over the effective running of the boat and ordered the depth to be reached or to resurface.

If after a few minutes, nothing happened, the boat rose to periscope depth upon the commander's orders. The engines were set to average speed, the planes set to rise and a certain amount of water was flushed out which made the vessel rise, decreasing the air pressure and making the vessel lighter which had to take on some ballast. The choice of the amount of ballast to take on was the role of the engineer who knew the exact quantities to take on according to, notably, the salinity of the water. The boat, with a positive angle of 10°, rose at a speed of one metre per second, a speed which was slow but necessary to stabilize at a depth of 20 metres in order to keep an under water stability at periscope depth of 15 metres. When periscope depth was rea-

entered the crash dive tanks and within a few seconds the water was noisily flushed out. Once empty, these tanks closed, the pressure caused by the compressed air was too strong and had to be compensated. The control room leading rate reduced the pressure by putting some the air in the submarine which ended up by increasing the atmospheric pressure inside the vessel. Once this operation had been carried out, the submarine was balanced, that is to say the last air reserves were pushed out of the ballast tanks. This was absolutely necessary as they could quickly become troubleso-

above

The watch officer was the last man to descend into the conning tower in an alert, sometimes hanging from the hatch in order to close it more quickly, it was, however, the commander who was the first to open it and climb onto the bridge. *(DR)*

below

Purging the ballasts at the start of a dive on U-552. *(ECPAD/DAM 1188 L29)*

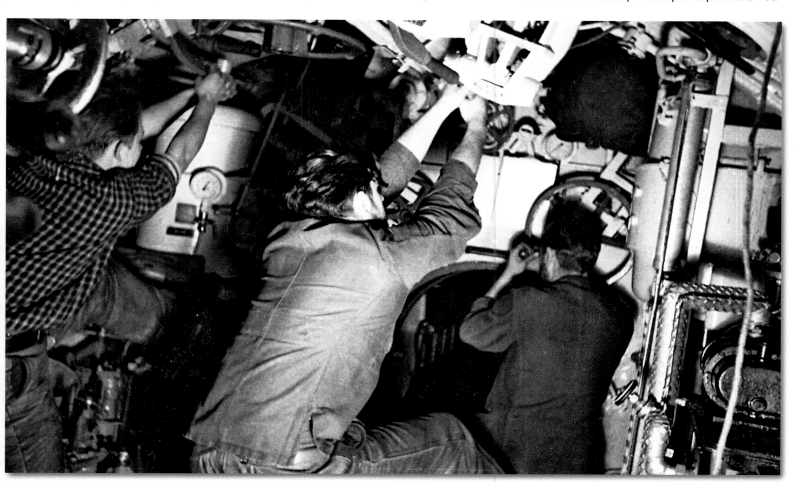

ched, the propellers turned slowly so that no bubbles would appear and that the periscope which barely appeared above water would not leave a visible wake.

The commander, in the control room, then quickly observed the horizon to decide whether to surface again or not. During this time, those who were to climb back up for the watch got ready to regain their posts in the « bathtub » by cleaning their binoculars. Once the order to regain the surface had been given, the men had to wait a few minutes more for the officer mechanic to balance the boat, sometimes by descending a little. Indeed, as the resurfacing manoeuvres demanded that certain men moved, this meant that the balance was affected. Water therefore had to pumped into the ballast tanks fore and aft to maintain a perfect trim. A mechanic, responsible for working the valves, pumped in this water very quickly according to the successive orders. This task demanded a remarkable level of skill that could only be acquired with practice.

Indeed, the wheels commanding

top left
A variation of the U-Boote war badge dating from the second half of the conflict. It is made from refined zinc and covered in a fairly fragile gilding.
(Militaria Magazine)

below
A case for the U-Boote war badge. At the beginning it was awarded in a case ; then as the war dragged on, in a box because of wartime austerity measures, some makers, such as Schwerin, simply put it in a brown envelope.
(P. de Romanovsky collection)

the valves were sometimes used to fill and sometimes to empty the trim tanks. The water was flushed to the ballast tanks on order.

After the chief engineer had announced that the conning tower hatch was above the water, the commander opened it, not without risk, because although in the absolute, the interior pressure had to be identical to that of the exterior, the reality was always different. If the interior pressure was too strong, the commander was brutally sucked out towards the exterior and could be injured, if it was too weak, opening the hatch required great strength. Once the hatch was open, the commander and the watch officer would leap onto the bridge and check the horizon whilst the

above
Maintenance on the ballast tanks on the outside of the hull, that are seen here open, showing the thick hull, was one of the essential tasks of the personnel. The ballast tanks were situated on the outside of the hull, fore and aft, and in the thick hull, under the central flooring. *(DR)*

boat continued to surface with the electric motors at full power to allow, in the case of immediate danger, to dive more quickly. At the same time, the exhaust fumes of the diesels which had been started, were used to flush out the remaining water in the ballast tanks (even if, theoretically, the latter could be flushed out with compressed air, it was preferable to save this as it could turn out to be vital in the case

left
An officer in the control room quickly checks the horizon.
(DR)

right
In the conning tower, the helmsman keeps his eyes fixed on the gyroscopic compass (Anschutz system) on his left. At full speed, with the wheel full over, the boat turned one metre every 10 seconds. In front of him, level with his forehead is the engine gauge.
(ECPAD/DAM 1248 L5)

previous page top
Disengaging the clutch of the diesels on what appears to be U-50, the insignia of which can be seen on the sailor's Bordmütze. This manoeuvre was essential during a crash dive. The man had to go from diesel propulsion to electric propulsion in a few seconds. This manoeuvre was sometimes carried out in an emergency during a « Stuka » dive during which the submarine dived with its diesel engines at full power for a faster dive and only stopped when the water reached the conning tower. It was at this point that the electric propulsion had to take over in order to maintain the speed that allowed the boat, with an angle which could reach 30), to quickly reach the depths.
(ECPAD/DAM 1081 L10)

of an accident for an emergency resurfacing. Furthermore, the exhaust fumes, loaded with greasy substances, helped maintain the ballast tanks). When a convoy was spotted, a powerful rangefinder (UZO or Überwasser Ziel Optik) was attached to a mount on the bridge. It allowed the calculation of the exact distance to the objective and as it was mechanically linked, like the periscope, to the torpedo launching mechanism ; it was used for surface attacks. The commander would then take over operations. He gave the position of the boat to be pursued and its distance from the submarine, a distance which could not exceed 16 nautical miles to avoid losing sight of it, and not less then 14 nautical miles because the

conning tower would could then be spotted by its prey.

During the pursuit, the whole crew was ready for action. The delicate mechanisms of the torpedoes were checked over by the torpedo officer and the diesels' control dials were checked to make sure that neither the radiator water temperature nor that of the exhaust fumes rose abnormally. Although the torpedoing of a convoy was the event for which eve-

U-9, emerges at a positive angle of between 25 and 30° for the benefit of the photographer, this was more spectacular than really useful. On the other hand, this angle when negative, enabled the boat, in the case of an alert, to gain a few seconds of dive which could ensure the crew's survival. *(P-M Rousseau collection)*

night. All the officers were on the bridge, assisted by the best lookouts, those whose eyesight had been rendered more piercing by hours of uninterrupted watches. They were not stood down, even if the chase lasted several days. The watch during the course of an attack was once more a particular trial. The lookouts only drank coffee, which was handed out individually so as not to distract more than one man at a time, and they only ate chocolate. The latter, called « for submariners », was particularly easy to digest so that their stomach was not overburdened, something which would increase their fatigue.

When night fell, the submarine got as close as possible to its target but not less than 5,000 metres to avoid the crest of its foam and wake from being spotted by the enemy. When the boat was close, compressed air was pushed into the ballast tanks at regular intervals, to allow the submarine to flush out as much water as possible and gain the speed it would need within the convoy and to get away without risk once the targets had been hit. Whilst the vessel bore down on its prey, the radio man found the international wavelengths so they could hear any eventual distress calls which would identify the sunk ship and the watertight hatches were checked for the eventuality of being attacked with depth charges. On the bridge or in the conning tower, alongside the commander, the first watch officer got ready to direct the torpedo launches. Thanks to the indications of his chief, he communicated the target's speed

ry man had rehearsed his role a hundred times during exercises, and the risk of human error was always possible, it was out of the question that the boat should fail in any way. At the same time, everything had to be in its place, the plates were washed, the bunks folded back and the flooring of the forward post was taken up to allow for rapid access to the reserve torpedoes. The loading arm for placing the torpedoes in the tubes was set at the right height so that they could be picked up and placed in the position for rapid loading in tubes 1 and 2, the explosive charges (and their detonators) were checked and set to explode in the event of scuttling. The sailors, finally, tore off the tally bearing the name of their flotilla from their caps in order to prevent revealing the boat's identity if captured by the enemy (this was no longer necessary after 1939 as they were replaced with a « Kriegsmarine » cap tally).

This scenario is obviously a model which only applied to specific operations such as that of Scapa Flow, and not for attacking convoys where events could unfold so quickly that these preparations could not be carried out. Although the hunt and pursuit were day time phases, the attack itself was carried out at

above
On board U-98, the man operating the rudder. On his right can be seen the ladder leading down from the bridge.
(ECPAD/DAM 944 L19)

above
Starter manometer of the diesel engine.
(P-M Rousseau collection)

right
Lifting a reserve torpedo on U-741.
(ECPAD/DAM 1033 L18)

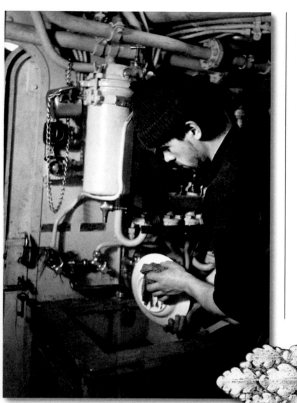

The torpedo officer had a device which took all of this information and automatically came up with the torpedoes' angle of gyro deviation, this was electronically transmitted to the torpedoes' direction system.

As long as the calculations were not finished, two red lights remained lit and when they went out, even if the submarine had, during this time, swerved, the setting would take these modifications into account as long as the target remained in the sights. When these final calculations had been carried out, the calculation device was attached to the tubes and the launch information, which varied, was automatically transmitted to the torpedoes. From this moment on, it was possible to fire from any position as long as the angle remained under 90°. As soon as the tubes were

and heading to the man operating the torpedo launch. Once the commander had given the order to prepare the launch, he put his night binoculars on the bridge sights and gave the final target details to the men who would launch the torpedo. Finally, he specified the angle to the objective, its speed, distance and the running depth for the torpedoes.

above
Although the commander of U-960 wears the legendary white cap, his first watch officer prefers a more practical and warmer woolly hat. Between the two men can be seen the automatic UZO torpedo aiming system for surface attacks, upon which were placed watch or firing binoculars, the system was linked to a firing calculator. The binoculars were orientated by the flange at the base.
(P-M Rousseau collection)

below
A wristwatch bearing the Kriegsmarine KM. Known makes for the navy are, Marton/Sigerin, Berg, Junghans.
(P-M Rousseau collection)

flooded and the valves opened by the wheel (at the last possible minute to prevent slowing down the boat), the engineer calculated the amount of water that he would have to pump or let into the submarine after the torpedo was launched in order to compensate the weight and maintain the boat's trim. When the torpedo room received the confirmation of a possible launch, the order to fire was given from the bridge or the conning tower. It was then passed to the control room which immediately sent it to the torpedo room, the accurate transmission of which the petty officer, in front of the calculator in the conning tower, could check thanks to the dull control light.

The commander specified next, to the torpedo officer, the submarine's speed and rotation when the rudder was fully turned to port or starboard. Whilst the submarine was turning, the calculation devices gave new numbers which corrected the adjustment of the torpedoes. The NCO in front of the calculation panel announced them, accompanied with the word « *covered* ». If the boat ever went outside the firing zone, a panel would light up with the words « *out of range* », indicating that the torpedoes could not reach their target.

In the torpedo room, the torpedo officer received his orders via headphones so that he could make up for an eventual break down in the electronic firing system manually. He stood up in front of the target optic, the UZO, and gave the order to launch, whilst at the same time pressing the launch button. The order, repeated by a petty officer, arrived via the microphone to the second torpedo man in the torpedo room. He had his hands on both of the torpedo activators of the two tubes and a foot placed on a third. The torpedoes were then launched and the compressed air pushed them out of the tubes, causing a brief muffled whistling sound. The torpedoes left the tubes one after another with an interval of one and two tenths of a second so as not to cause each other any problems. Once launched, the compressed air used to push the torpedoes out was reabsorbed with an enormous jet of water. The torpedoes then ran at the required depth, more often between five and seven metres below the surface and passing under the enemy ship, ideally two metres under the keel in order to set off the magnetic pistol which activated the explosive charge, lifting the ship which would break in two as it came back down. As soon as the torpedo hit its target, the commander ordered a new heading whilst the torpedoes were replaced in the tubes. At the same time, the submarine moved away on the surface to avoid being spotted and to avoid the eddies that could pull the submarine down which were caused by the explosions of ships loaded with dynamite or petrol. In the more and more frequent case of escorts, the submarine dived so that it could observe its work through the periscope, whilst the commander kept his eyes fixed on his stopwatch which allowed him to estimate the speed.

At 400 metres, a torpedo took 25 seconds to hit its target but it was not uncommon, when the target was far away, or if the torpedoes took a long time to find it, for several minutes to go by before they hit their objective. When the merchant ship was hit, the whole crew was informed via the microphone equipment, they were allowed to come and take a look through the periscope. If the ship did not sink immediately, the commander did not hesitate in launching another attack, often at a much closer distance, sometimes less than 400 metres, diving under the target so that it

right
Victory pennant.
The minimum tonnage
for tanker was generally
around 6,000 metric tons.

left
A lookout using the telephone
in the conning tower on his way
to, or from, the bridge.
(ECPAD/DAM 944 L9)

below
At night, the destruction
of Allied ships appears to
the men of the submarine,
who are invited to come and
watch the show, like a scene of
the apocalypse, all the more so
when it is an oil tanker whose
holds, when they explode,
spread the burning oil over
the sea.
(ECPAD/DAM 964 L16)

whilst, although alcohol was forbidden, each man was allowed a mouthful of cognac.

Indeed, music played an essential role in the crew's morale, each submarine carried up to a hundred records, taken on board by officers who lived in France or Germany, but also by the crew. Music included the more famous classical pieces which were liked by everyone, such as Beethoven's *Overture in F minor: Egmont*, Mozart's *A Little Night-Music*, Liszt's *Préludes*, Wagner's *opera Overtures* as well as German operetta songs. The collection had, of course, some traditional marching songs, but they were not always liked by everyone. The crew of U-505 had no scruples in changing the classic Prussian *Yorkscher Marsch* by the romantic song *Valencia*. However, popular music and dances were also largely appreciated as witnessed by the large number of tango, fox-trot and waltz records, as well as « hits » by German artists such as Teddy Stauffer, Zarah Leander, Marika Rökk,

could attack from the other side. When the torpedoes were all used up or the targets sunk, the crew could take a breather and were often allowed to relax for while. Diving to 50 metres to avoid the radars, the commander used the microphone once more to play records

Although legend has immortalised torpedo attacks, many of the Allied ships were sunk with the deck gun in order to save the precious « eels ». The photo here shows the slow death of the American steamer *Ruth Lykes*, attacked by U-103 on May 17th, 1942.
(ECPAD/DAM 969 L2)

Firing against a floating target with the flak gun, probably a 37 mm.
(ECPAD/DAM 965 L5)

A crew member with one of the five microphones on board, gives a general broadcast.
(ECPAD/DAM 1062 L25)

ced by some Glenn Miller. If the commander was too rigid or followed the rules to the letter, crew members did not hesitate in finding a way around the rules. When approaching the American coast, if the commander was asleep and despite his strict ban, the radio man would tune into the New York or Washington radio stations to get the jazz programmes.

However, most of the time, the moments following an attack were marked by an extreme tension. Firing from a few hundred metres meant running the risk of being detected ; the boat was no longer protected by the night due to the development of the radar. When the escorts arrived on the scene, they scanned the depths with their ASDIC which reverberated against the metal sides with the crisp sound of the sonar wave whilst the propellers swished overhead. As soon as the submarine was sure of having been detected it no longer had the time to play dead. The crew was like a well oiled machine and the boat descended full speed at a 40° angle, as quietly as possible. The electric motors turned at low power, orders were murmured, the auxiliary machines stop-

Lale Andersen and Evelyn Künnecke. The chief mechanic of U-612 owned a record by the latter, singing *Sing, Nachtigall, Sing*, a tune that was so popular that room was always left at mooring between boats so that the men could hear through the hatches and the conning tower. When the record was broken, the pieces were stuck back together so that some songs could still be played.

Jazz was also very popular but it was very difficult to get hold of records as it was banned in Germany. Some boats nevertheless had some records, U-515 was lucky in that the commander had been in the merchant navy and had managed to build up a good collection of Cole Porter records before war broke out. For those less lucky, and despite the fact that it was forbidden to listen to enemy radio stations, commanders often turned a blind eye, if only to be able to obtain information on comrades who had been taken prisoner, information which was often spa-

above
Sailors could purchase this type of mouth organ at the Soldatenheim (soldier's residence)
(ECPAD/DAM 1062 L25)

below
A submariners' march and song begging women left behind on dry land to remain faithful to the men gone « to the blue sea ». *(DR)*

above
After a successful torpedo attack, the crew members of U-103 fish out crates containing the cargo of the sunken ship. Although the crates might not have contained anything of use to the men on board, certain items could be kept as trophies or souvenirs.
(ECPAD/DAM 964 L3)

ped and the sailors put on their felt shoes. The American admiral, Gallery, in charge of a group of escorts specialised in anti-submarine warfare, said after the war that, « *the noise of a coffee cup falling on a submerged submarine's metal floor could be heard by a destroyer passing overhead and an oil pump which was a little noisy would sound like a fire alarm bell to the destroyer's listening device* ».

For moving around, the watch officer had to be informed, notably when passing through the control room, to avoid unbalancing the boat. However, generally speaking, those who had nothing to do were sent to lie down to economize the air, a precaution which could turn out to be vital, no one knew when the pursuit would end... (it could last for more than 48 hours, a period after which the submarine had to resurface). The explosion of the first depth charge produced a thud that reverberated throughout the boat. Despite the fear that could grip the men, no one could move as it could result in upsetting the delicate balance of the submarine, shouting was also out of the question to avoid it being picked up on the surface. Immediately after the explosion, the three compartments (aft, central and fore) reported any damage.

When the depth charges began to get closer, men were thrown about by the shockwaves. Under the effect of this hammering on the hull, barometers and gauges cracked and lights shattered, plunging the boat into darkness before the emergency lighting began working. The team of electricians went though the boat repairing and plugging the lighting into the second electrical network. When the explosions were thirty metres away, the situation became critical. Leaks appeared and water began to stream into the boat, indeed the slightest crack at this depth had to resist the water pressure whilst at the same time being very difficult to block up. From this moment on, the light bulbs were not even replaced even though the darkness increased the fear. The submarine could then descend to the « cellar » up to 250 metres, beyond this depth the metal walls between the armoured sections, would begin to buckle, threatening to give way at any moment. The reason for this dive came from the lesser precision of depth charges beyond 150 metres due to their being set off by timer fuse and not by a pressure sensitive membrane. However, with the improvements made to ASDIC, the escorts could in any case follow a submarine for a long time and keep its head below water.

If, thanks to the skill of the commander, the submarine managed to escape from the

above
An escort launches a depth charge against a U-Boot.
(DITE/USIS)

The Hedgehog which permitted the launching of salvos of explosives.
(DITE/USIS)

escorts' intensive depth charging, it had to surface as quickly as possible to recharge the battery accumulators in order to be able to make another emergency dive. As soon as the submarine broke surface, the diesels were started at full speed at the same whilst the two compressors filled the bottles of compressed air. The ventilators cleared the air inside and all the hatches were opened so that the vacuum effect of the diesels accelerated the intake of fresh air. In one hour, the boat's air was renewed. So that combat readiness could be maintained at all times, the men took two caffeine and pervitin tablets which allowed them to stay awake for several days.

Win or die

At a depth of less than 50 metres, a submarine damaged by depth charges was extremely vulnerable to being detected but could still surface and remain afloat long enough to evacuate the crew. At more than 50 metres, the water pressure would flood the boat too quickly to get every one out. The boat would then flood very quickly and at a greater speed the deeper it descended due to the increased pressure, until the latter crushed the hull. In the event of the disappearance of a submarine, the high command did not release the news until six months had passed. Trapped, hunted by the escorts' ASDIC when submerged, and by the radars when on the surface, the U-Boote fought with the energy of despair,

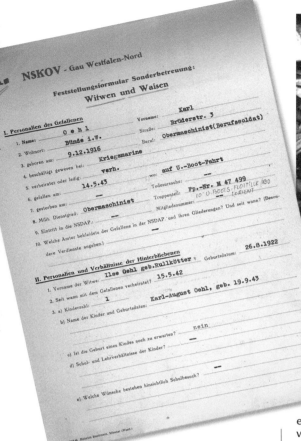

Each one of the he electric engines was capable of 375 HP. *(ECPAD/DAM 946 L13)*

above
At the beginning of a dive, the men on diesel engine watch closed the exhaust valves which opened onto the exterior. As with all air vents, the valves had to be closed immediately when the boat dived. *(DR)*

top left
An information form concerning the widow and child of Obermaschinist Karl Oehl, lost on May 14th, 1943 aged 27. It is probably information necessary for the payment of the pension. *(P. de Romanovsky collection)*

below
After the explosion of a depth charge, every man had to check that no leak had appeared or worsened. *(DR)*

accumulated in the air and prevented the 4 % limit, which would kill a man, from being passed. Despite this, the slightest movement required an energy that, very quickly, no man was able to find. The air, which had become damp, deadened the men's senses who had to remain at their posts and who could not go and quench their thirst.

It is certain that submariners could live for a long time after their boat had been hit and their agony could be prolonged if the pressure did not crush the sides of the hull. Everything, therefore, was in the hands of the commander whose decisions decided if his crew lived or died. These decisions were difficult to take and, sometimes, to be accepted by young officers, barely convinced by their commander's decision to surrender in order to save the crew. Filled with all the ideals of heroic sacrifice, they preferred to scuttle, or sometimes die, rather than be dishonoured by their capture, or worst still that of their boat. Councils of

with the hunt lasting a very long time. U-358 was chased for 38 hours by four British escorts from February 29th, 1944 until it was finally sunk along with its crew on March 1st (there was one survivor) by *HMS Affleck*, having managed to sink *HMS Gould*. After being hunted for 24 hours, air became scarce inside the boat and the men were sent to their bunks. They then breathed through rubber tubes connected to potassium filters. The one kilogram filter absorbed the carbon dioxide which

honour, held in P.O.W. camps are a good example of this mentality, which lead to the banishment of he who had failed in his duty, such as in the case of commander Rahmlow, judged by his peers in a Canadian P.O.W. camp.

However, if the commander considered that he had fought well, and that it was no longer possible to fight on without being sunk, it was not uncommon that he accepted to surrender. Even an « ace » like Kretschmer, commander of U-99, after diving to 220 metres, with no means of fighting back, and incapable of manoeuvring correctly, decided to surface and surrender, not without having put into place the self destruction devices. In this event, the submarine had two hatches for scuttling, one in the forward post, the other under the electric motors, these could sink the submarine in ten minutes. Explosives could also be placed in various compartments and booby traps (wires, placed in the control room, linked to

above
In one of the two batteries, an electrician measures the electrolyte acidity of the accumulators to determine the battery's state of charge. He is lying on a small trolley that can move backwards or forwards. Because of the low height of the ceiling, the accumulators were placed under the flooring of the gangway.
(ECPAD/DAM 1062 L26)

left
Opening the valves to scuttle the boat. Illustration by Tress.
(ECPAD/DAM 1515 L2)

right
In the control room, the helmsman at the controls of the dive planes. In front of him is the depth gauge. Behind him is the rudder control.
(ECPAD/DAM 1232 L33)

left
A letter announcing to the parents the loss at sea of their son « *for the Führer and the Fatherland* » and asking them not to make an announcement in the newspaper so as not to inadvertently inform the intelligence services of the Allied countries.
(F. Bachmann collection)

below
Cap insignia of U-313.
(Private coll.)

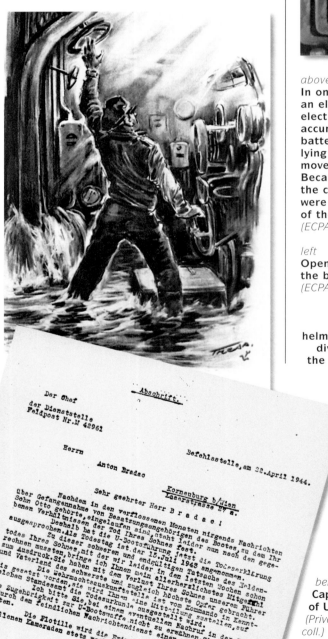

the torpedo pistols) set in the event of an enemy boarding party. In theory, the commander had to remain below to insure that all the secret documents were destroyed. Some did not have the time to do this, or in the general panic, forgot to do it. It was thanks to this sort of

forgetfulness that the Allies managed to get their hands on an Enigma machine and its precious codes, abandoned by commander Lemp during the emergency evacuation, convinced that *HMS Bulldog*, which was speeding towards him was going to ram the submarine. Even if the drill had been practised countless times, no one could guarantee, with the damage which the submarine had often already suffered, that the explosions would go off and that the boat would sink in time. In the case of Kretschmer's U-99, the chief engineer went back below to flood the ballast tanks and perished along with two of his companions. Some were luckier, such as the two men in charge of scuttling U-269 in June 1944. Officer mechanic Mürb and second mate Jaburek were trapped in the control room as the boat was sinking, they were lucky that it settled at a depth of 60 metres. After having closed themselves in the conning tower, they opened the upper hatch and managed to regain the surface. Even if the equipment destined for getting out of their steel coffin was basic, the submariners managed in this way to escape. This was notably the case of U-413 which, when it was hit in the English Channel on August 20th, 1944, settled on the sea bed at a depth of 27 metres and from which the chief engineer managed to escape, rising to the surface in an air bubble which gave him a little oxygen. The most

above
A later version of the U-Boote war badge, it is a well made woven version in gilded aluminium thread.
(Militaria Magazine)

as they climbed up. Those who reached the surface could climb into inflatable dinghies, stored in the superstructure and which had been released from the inside.

U-Boote could also fall victim to human error, even though everything was done to avoid it. It is estimated that roughly 5 % of losses were caused by diving accidents or collisions. In 1941, U-331 launched a spread of torpedoes at a distance of 375 metres from the cruiser *Barham* and ordered a crash dive. However, the sudden loss of weight, due to the torpedoes leaving the tubes, which was not compensated in time by the chief engineer, made it surface where it was rammed by the *Valiant* which tore off its conning tower. It managed, despite everything, to dive to a depth that it thought was 80 metres and waited. However, due to a crew member's negligence, the manometer was stuck and the real depth was in fact 266 metres where it could have been crushed at any moment by the pressure. In August 1944, an error by the radio

above
A large oil slick... from 1943, the life expectancy of a submarine was now only two campaigns. The crews were exhausted by the frequency of missions that they carried out and the officers were increasingly less experienced and less well trained.
(IWM)

incredible rescue was certainly that of a petty officer who managed to escape via the conning tower hatch of U-1199 in January 1945, from a depth of 73 metres.

The situation was more critical when an entire crew had to evacuate a boat on the seabed. Equipped with their Dräger Tauchretter (a life jacket which allowed them to breath under water), the men, who had learned how to use it in a specially built tank on land, went into the conning tower and opened the hatches in order to get to the surface as quickly as possible, holding hands so that no one would be lost whilst the commander counted his men

operator of U-534, the last U-Boot which managed to escape from Bordeaux, almost led to a catastrophe. At the first emergency dive, the portable radio device on the bridge used for detecting the enemy, blocked the aerial in the rungs of the conning tower ladder, preventing the second from passing. The latter sacrificed himself and ordered the closure of the control room hatch and to dive. Despite everything, he avoided drowning thanks to the pressure which ended up closing the conning tower hatch on the bridge.

When a submarine was sunk by a surface ship, the survivors were picked up. The situa-

DEPTH CHARGING OF THE U-977

« *It was a fine day, but not too good for us, for the sea was glassily calm, perfect for their ASDIC. A report came from the hydrophone operator:*

"*Propellers at high speed. Probably destroyers. Trying to pick us up on their ASDICS*".

"*Dive to 75 fathoms. Silent speed.*"

We were all ready, with our felt shoes on and all but the most essential lighting shut off to save current, as we had no idea how long the hunt would last. The enemy were in triangular formation, with us in the middle, and I must say they worked superbly. We had never known the first charges to fall with such uncomfortable accuracy as these did, invariably six at a time. All the glass panels on our controls were shattered and the deck was strewn with splinters. Valve after valve loosened, and before long the water came trickling through. The attack went on unremittingly for three hours without a break, the charges falling thicker and thicker around us, cruising as we were now at a depth of 100 fathoms. With the need to save current we were working the hydroplane and the steering gear by hand, and meanwhile the hydrophone was picking up more destroyers, though only the men within earshot knew it. What was the point of upsetting the others?

Faces are pale, and every forehead sweating. We all know what the other man's thinking. There are six destroyers now, three of them heading for Gibraltar,
but fresh ones always coming up in relay. Like this they'll never run out of depth-charges- our position's truly desperate, the fine weather dead against us. Why doesn't the storm blow up, like it always did when we were on our way here?*

By the time we have had sixteen hours of it we have long given up counting the depth- charges. During this time no one's had any sleep, and we've all dark rings under our eyes. Plenty of bulbs have broken, but we don't change them — with the emergency lighting we can only guess the position of the various installations. The darkness makes it all the more frightening.

There've been tricky moments before, but this time it's just hell. At times we have to dive to 126 fathoms. The steel bulkhead supports are buckling and may give at any moment. But perhaps just because of this we are calm.

"*Well, it's not everyone who gets such an expensive coffin*" *a dry voice remarks.*

"*Four million marks it cost*".

Yes, when it happens it'll be quick enough.

If only we could defend ourselves, see something to shoot at — the sense of being trapped into inactivity is unbearable. The current is down to danger level, the compressed air cylinders almost empty and the air itself tastes leaden. Our oxygen is scarce, our carbon monoxide content continually increasing, so that we're breathing with difficulty like so many marathon runners in the last mile; at this rate we can last out twenty hours
longer then we'll just have to surface. We know what will happen then, we've read the dispatches: as soon as the U-boat surfaces, all the warships open fire, and the bombardment goes on even though the crew have begun to jump overboard- they must be made to lose their nerve and forget to sink their boat. It was one of the enemy's dearest wishes to capture a U-boat, as that would have made it so much easier to devise means of countering the German underwater threat.*

"*Stand by for depth charge attack!*" *They are falling right alongside now. A roar and a crash in the control room enough to crack our eardrums- fragments of iron around — valves smash to bits. In spite of oneself one can't help stretching a hand out towards one's escape gear. The petty officer in the control room has his hand on the flood valve to let in compressed air for surfacing, but he's awaiting the commander's order, and all the time they are still thundering at us. The helmsman shouts that the compass has been blown out of its frame with its 10,000 revolutions a minute the gyro wheel goes spinning round the boat, but luckily none of us is hit.*

In a council of war with the officers, the commander admitted the situation was pretty hopeless; it might even be that we should have to surface and sink the boat. On the other hand the moon would not rise until two in the morning and it would be dark till then- if we surfaced in the dark, there was just still a hundred to one chance we might break out of the trap that

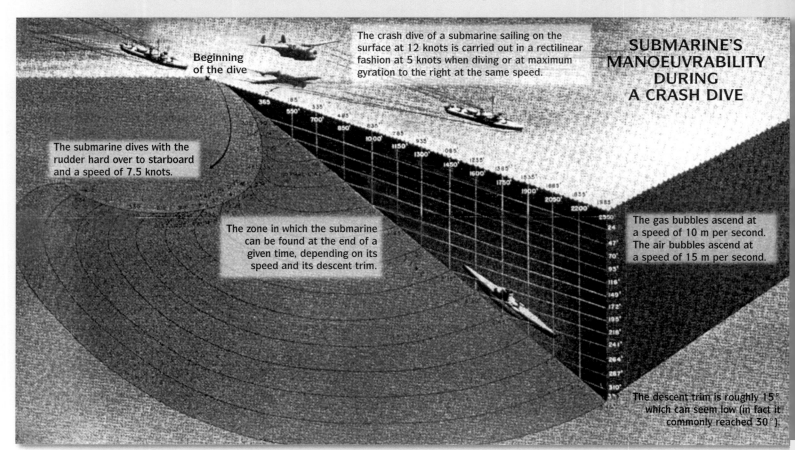

Beginning of the dive

The crash dive of a submarine sailing on the surface at 12 knots is carried out in a rectilinear fashion at 5 knots when diving or at maximum gyration to the right at the same speed.

SUBMARINE'S MANOEUVRABILITY DURING A CRASH DIVE

The submarine dives with the rudder hard over to starboard and a speed of 7.5 knots.

The zone in which the submarine can be found at the end of a given time, depending on its speed and its descent trim.

The gas bubbles ascend at a speed of 10 m per second. The air bubbles ascend at a speed of 15 m per second.

The descent trim is roughly 15° which can seem low (in fact it commonly reached 30°).

way. Meanwhile everything was ready to blow up the boat. Time fuses were laid against the torpedo warheads and in other vulnerable places all over the ship so that if one didn't explode there was every chance that another would. In no circumstances must we fall into enemy hands and as a result be responsible for the deaths of many fellow U-boat men. Next we distributed escape gear and lifeboats — a one man collapsible rubber dinghy per head. The commander and bridge watch put on red glasses to accustom their eyes to the dark so that they should be able to see the moment that we surfaced — I couldn't help thinking this superfluous, for inside the boat it was as good as pitch dark anyhow. Next the ASDIC decoys were thrown out, and we began to fill balloons with metal strips attached which were to be released when we surfaced to float low over the water and fox the enemy radar. As we prepared to surface at 50 fathoms we caught the sound of ASDICS even more distinctly. Dam it, they'd still got us! As we shot up to 25 fathoms we could hear loud explosions. The hydrophone operator announced :

"Destroyers at close quarters. Six different propellers turning."

Swearing, the commander gave the order to surface. By now we couldn't make full speed as the batteries weren't up to it. We brought up ammunition for the AA guns, large magazines with fifty rounds in each. Five torpedo tubes could fire simultaneously, and so could four machine guns. The belts of these latter did not give out like they do on machine guns ashore, but stretching right down into the control room, were constantly replenished so as to fire between them 6,400 rounds a minute. We could turn them on like hoses. Up to 2,000 metres we could menace a destroyer and outside 2,000 metres the destroyer couldn't spot us. Yet we knew that if it did come to an engagement we should certainly get the worst of it. We just hoped that we would not have to open fire and might get away unnoticed.

We drove to the surface as depth charges were still dropping around us. The ASDIC decoys were obviously fulfilling their purpose. All of a sudden the conning tower hatch burst open and we almost shot out of it. The pressure was terrific. The commander looked out to port and I to starboard. Thank heaven it was a dark night and the sky was overcast. We made out three destroyers, one 100 metres away at most, still dropping depth charges. We started up both diesel engines and rang down full speed at once- no time to let them warm up. The generators were gong too, as we had to recharge our batteries, besides the two compressors recharging the compressed air cylinders. The fans began to drive fresh air though the boat. The fresh air tore into our lungs :

we could hardly stand up and were practically fainting. Guns and machine guns were loaded and trained on the nearest destroyer, but we all hoped it wouldn't sight us for both our sakes. We had a new type of torpedo that could zig-zag or make circular tracks, but we weren't starting anything. Had we done so we couldn't have got away unmolested, since we lacked a good supply of two essentials ; current and compressed air. The range started to increase and the ten gas filled balloons we had released went up and drifted with the wind. The enemy radar would be amazed to pick up so many U-boats all at once. He presumably suspected the presence of still more where the ASDIC decoys were in action. We could well imagine the sort of radar activity going on just then on the bridge of one of these destroyers : Radar operator : "Ship bearing 040 degrees, range 6,000 metres. Fifteen more echoes on various bearings."

Destroyer Captain : "Plot the position of the hunting group and put on the chart". Navigator : "Instructions carried out". Captain. "Course so-and-so. Report radar bearings continuously." The destroyer approaches its target (a balloon). Searchlights are sweeping. The radar echo

fades out and the range is now under 1,000 metres, the minimum range of the radar sets of that time. Guns swing round-nothing to be seen, for the wires hanging from the balloons are very thin. Radar operator : "Echo right astern, probably the same object". Captain : " B-! We've overshot. Keep a better look out there ! These damned U-boats are too small. Might well slip a fish into us into the bargain. Hard a starboard ! "

At last we lost sight of the destroyers. The enemy radar was confused by all the echoes, and even if the destroyers did pick us out in the dark they could not go all out after us for fear of ramming other British ships.

After an hour we had taken in fresh air enough to cruise underwater for sixteen hours, and in two hours we were all fit for duty again though terribly exhausted. We dived to 50 fathoms and left Gibraltar as far away and as fast as we could. I though of the proverb, " When an ass steps on thin ice he generally falls through." Our ice had certainly been thin enough. »

Heinz Schaeffer : « U-Boat 977 » — Cerberus Publishing Ltd. 2003, ISBN 1 84145 027 8.

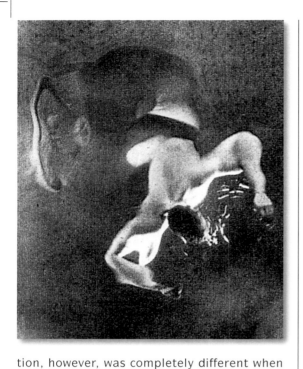

left
**In spite of the evacuation
exercises from the diving bell,
which permitted to reach very
great depths, in reality an
evacuation remained very
uncertain.**
(DR)

right
**The Dräger Tauchretter
(breathing apparatus equipped
with a life jacket, allowed a man
to breathe underwater),
nicknamed the « artificial lung ».**
(DR)

below
**A post card sent from Canada
to Germany by a Kapitänleutnant
in a PoW camp (camp 44) near
Ottawa, Canada in 1944.**
(P-M Rousseau collection)

tion, however, was completely different when
an attack was carried out by aircraft. Although
the plane could drop an inflatable dinghy, it often had to abandon the survivors but not without having signal-
led their position. Some men spent a
long time in the sea before being rescued. This was notably the case of commander Müller and a man from the crew
of U-662 who spent 17 days at sea
following an attack by a plane off the Bra-
zilian coast in July 1943. In the November of the same year, the sole survivor of
U-848, sunk south west of Ascension Island,
was fished out of the water
by the cruiser *USS Mar-
blehead* after having drifted for 30 days. Delirious
and almost dehydrated,
he only lived for a few
days after.

In the same way, the
attitude that a com-
mander had to adopt
concerning survivors
was far from that
which legend would
make us believe.

It is true, with one exception, that is has never been clearly proven that Allied survivors were machine gunned by a German submarine in the North Atlantic. There were cases of projectiles falling in the middle of the lifeboats during an attack on a convoy, but they were not necessarily aimed at the survivors, even if the latter were convinced that they were. There is a paradox here as Dönitz's orders were clear and left little space for interpretation. That the commanders forbade themselves from doing it is one thing, it is however, not sure that all refused to carry it out. After the war, when Kretschmer was entrusted with the care of the German Navy war memorial at Kiel by the president of Schleswig-Holstein, the latter proclaimed that « fighting at sea was waged with chivalry and was without hate (and that) the sea will always be a common link between the sailors of every nation », he was perhaps a little quick to agree with what submariners wished to make people believe post war.

It is in effect very clear in orders given by Dönitz, that any action contrary to interna-

previous page bottom
A U-Boot attacked by an American Avenger torpedo plane based on an escort aircraft carrier. *(National Archives)*

above
Cap insignia of U-26.
(P. de Romanovsky collection)

ional law should not be written down in the log books, the famous Kriegestagebuch, but only mentioned verbally upon returning to base. Choosing to leave the survivors of a merchant ship, notably near the American coast, meant that they would be immediately picked up and made available once again to crew another ship as well as being able to alert the presence of a submarine. Without passing judge-

above
The survivors of a sunken submarine cling onto large buoys. *(IWM)*

Top right:
Dönitz forbade that any action contrary to international law be mentioned in the log books.
(P-M Rousseau collection)

ment on what may have happened and without giving too much credence to myth (especially given the fact that the Americans did not act any differently in the Pacific with Japanese ships), this reality allows us to understand how submarine warfare, in all its aspects which its techniques imposed on it, was part of the process of total war where the destruction of the enemy was consubstantial to victory. ❏

ACKNOWLEDGEMENTS

This work owes much to those classic works essential to those who seek to know the living conditions of German submariners during the Second World War. Beyond Léonce Peillard's classics, we must mention here the major work of Thimothy P. Mulligan which revives the genre and provides precious information, often previously unknown, gathered during remarkable and thorough archive work ; his work deserves our recognition as we used it to shed light on many points of essential detail. The work of those responsible for the u-boat.net website must also be mentioned as it teems with precious information, indispensable for German submarine enthusiasts. But this work could never have come into being without the active participation of the vessel captain Bernard Labit, ex-commanders of the *Argonaute*, the editing skills of Alexandre Thers, the kindness of Pierre-Marie Rousseau, who made many photographs, documents and historical souvenirs from his collection available to me, as did Pascal de Romanovsky, specialist of the Russian Imperial Navy and Franck Bachmann, specialist of the Kriegsmarine. I would like to thank them warmly for their precious help.

BIBLIOGRAPHY

- Jacques Alaluquetas : *U-Boot VII-C. Technique, construction, armement*, Paris, Grancher, 2004.
- Karl Alman : *Les Loups gris dans la mer bleue*, Paris, Presses de la Cité, 1968.
- Jean-Jacques Antier : *Les sous-mariniers*, Rennes, Editions Ouest France, 1994.
- Breyer Siegfried, Koop Gerhard : *The German navy at War 1939-1945*. Vol. 2. *The U-Boat*, Schiffer publishing, 1989.
- Lothar-Gunther Bucheim : *Le Bateau*, Paris, Albin Michel, 1977.
- Harald Busch : *Meutes sous-marines*, Paris, France-Empire, 1952.
- Cajus Bekker : *Mer maudite. Journal de guerre de la marine allemande*, Paris, France-Empire, 1971.
- Douglas Botting : *Les sous-marins allemands*, Paris, Editions Time Life, 1979.
- Jochen Brennecke : *Le destin tragique des sous-mariniers allemands*, Paris, Editions France-Empire, 1974.
- Grand Amiral Dönitz : *La guerre en quarante questions*, Paris, La Table Ronde, 1969.
- Grand Amiral Dönitz : *Dix ans et vingt jours*, Paris, Plon, 1959.
- Wolfgang Franak : *U-Boote contre les marines alliées*, Paris, Arthaud, 1956.
- De Gmeline Patrick : *Sous-marins allemands au combat 1939-1945*, Paris, Presses de la Cité , 1997.
- Jack Mallmann Showell : *Wolfpacks at war. The U-Boat experience in the World War II*, London, Ian Allan Publishing, 2001.
- David Miller : *U-Boats. History, development and equipment 1914-1945*, London, Pegasus Publishing, 2000.
- Thimothy P Mulligan : *Neither sharks nor wolves. The Men of nazi Germany's U-Boat Arm 1939-1945*, Naval Institute Press, Annapolis, Maryland, 1999.
- Jean Noli : *Les loups de l'amiral. Les sous-marins allemands dans la bataille de l'Atlantique*, Paris, Fayard, 1970.
- Peter Padfield : *Dönitz et la guerre des U-Boote*, Paris, Pygmalion, 1986.
- Léonce Peillard : *La bataille de l'Atlantique*, T. I et II, Paris, Robert Laffont, 1974.
- Léonce Peillard : *Histoire générale de la guerre sous-marine 1939-1945*, Paris, Robert Laffont, 1970.
- Anthony Preston : *U-Boote. L'histoire des sous-marins allemands*, Paris, Fernand Nathan, 1979.
- Grand Amiral Raeder : *Ma vie*, Paris, France Empire, 1958.
- Terence Robertson : *Sous-marin d'attaque*, Paris, Jacques Grancher éditeur, 1983.
- Heinz Schaeffer : *U-977. L'odyssée d'un sous-marin allemand*, Paris, Julliard, 1952.
- Herbert Werner : *Dix-huit secondes pour survivre*, Paris, Robert Laffont, 1970.
- J-P Dallies-Labourdette : *U-Boote 1935-1945*, Paris, Histoire & Collections, 1996.
- J-P Dallies-Labourdette : *S-Boote 1939-1945*, Paris, Histoire & Collections, 2003.

Design, creation, lay-out, illustration research and direction by Alexandre THERS, with the help of Thibaut PANFILI and Aurore MATHIEU
© Histoire & Collections 2007

ISBN : 978-2-35250-046-9

Publisher's number : 35250

© Histoire & Collections 2007

HISTOIRE & COLLECTIONS
SA au capital de 182 938, 82 €
5, avenue de la République
F-75541 Paris Cédex 11 - France
Tel : 01 40 21 18 20
Fax : 01 47 00 51 11
Internet : www.histoireetcollections.com

This book has been designed, typed, laid-out and processed by Histoire & Collections and 'le Studio Graphique A & C' on fully integrated computer equipment.
Color separation : Studio A & C
Printed by MCC Graphics, Spain, EEC
August 2007